THE COMPLETE GUIDE TO
U.S. PRESIDENTS

An Imprint of Sterling Publishing
1166 Avenue of The Americas
New York, NY, 10036

Text © 2015 by QEB Publishing, Inc.
Illustrations © 2015 by QEB Publishing, Inc.

Design: Jessica Moon and Paul Myerscough
Editorial: Amanda Learmonth and Sarah Eason
Picture Research: Susannah Jayes

This 2015 edition published by Sandy Creek.

ISBN 978-1-4351-6169-6

Manufactured in China
Lot #:
2 4 6 8 10 9 7 5 3
11/15

THE COMPLETE GUIDE TO
U.S. PRESIDENTS

JODIE PARACHINI

Sandy Creek
NEW YORK

CONTENTS

Words in **bold** are explained in the Glossary on page 140.

E PLURIBUS UNUM

THE CREATION OF THE UNITED STATES

"We hold these truths to be self-evident, that all men are created equal, that they are endowed by their Creator with certain unalienable Rights, that among these are Life, Liberty and the pursuit of Happiness."

In 1776, a group of leaders known as the **Founding Fathers of America** declared that they wanted to form a new nation, separate from the British Empire that ruled over them. The men wrote down a list of grievances, or complaints, to King George III. On July 4, 1776, the Founding Fathers stated they would no longer be ruled by Britain in the **Declaration of Independence.** The United States was born.

American Revolution

The American **colonies** had been at war with Britain for a year when the Declaration of Independence was signed. However, the battle for independence would take a bit longer. America had assembled a Continental Army—led by Commander-in-Chief George Washington—to fight the **American Revolution**, a war that would last until 1783.

Washington leading the Continental Army into battle against the British.

Establishing a Government

Once the American Revolution was won, the new nation set about forming a **government.** Should national hero George Washington become a king like the **monarchy** in Great Britain? If not, who should have all the power to make decisions and control the people? These were the questions that the new nation faced.

In 1777, the nation formed its own flag, with 13 red and white stripes and 13 stars, representing the 13 states.

FAST FACTS

Instead of a monarchy, the United States would become a **democracy** and **elect** a President every four years.

The Founding Fathers signing the Declaration of Independence.

WHO WAS FIRST?

The British were not the first people to live on the land now known as America. It is thought that the first inhabitants may have crossed over the Bering Land Bridge that connected Siberia (Russia) to Alaska. Thousands of years later, American Indian tribes roamed the land, well before the Spanish and Christopher Columbus "discovered" the New World in the 15th century.

THE NEW CONSTITUTION

In 1787, a set of laws was written down that described the way the new United States government would be formed. That document, the **Constitution**, lists the rights and responsibilities given to the states, as well as the framework, or structure, for a central, **federal** government.

Independence Hall in Philadelphia is the site where both the Declaration of Independence and the Constitution were approved.

The Rights of the People

The Constitution doesn't mention the individual rights of the **citizens**. So, in 1791, statesman James Madison suggested 12 **amendments** known as the **Bill of Rights**. Ten were approved, including the right for people to practice any religion, to say what they believe, and to gather together to express ideas.

The Bill of Rights was approved on December 15, 1791.

WHO CAN BE PRESIDENT?

- ✓ U.S. citizens
- ✓ People over 35 years old
- ✓ Residents of the United States for more than 14 years

Separation of Powers

The Constitution says that the United States will have three "branches" of government (think of it like a tree). There will be a President who will be the head of the Executive branch; there will be a group of leaders from each state to join the **Congress**, who will lead the Legislative branch; and special judges on the Supreme Court will guide the Judicial branch. The laws create a series of **checks and balances** so that no one person or branch has more power than the others.

Executive branch

Legislative branch

Judicial branch

More Changes

Over the years, amendments have been proposed to help clarify what was meant in the Constitution.

These include:

• The Thirteenth Amendment: the abolishment of slavery (1865)

• The Fifteenth Amendment: the right to vote shall not be denied to anyone based on race or color (1870)

• The Nineteenth Amendment: the right to vote shall not be denied to women (1920)

African American former slaves received the right to vote when the Fifteenth Amendment was approved in 1870.

POLITICAL PARTIES

Each American President (except George Washington) has been linked with a political party. Political parties are groups of people that have similar views about how the country should be run.

Each party has a different idea about:

• how to **tax** citizens

• how to spend the money that it raises

• how much control should be given to the federal government, as opposed to the government run by each of the states

Democratic-Republican

Thomas Jefferson was the first Democratic-Republican President. He organized this party to challenge and oppose the Federalist party. The four Presidents who ran as Democratic-Republicans distrusted the British and wanted less federal power.

John Adams (President No. 2), 1797–1801

Thomas Jefferson (President No. 3), 1801–1809.

Federalist

The Federalists were committed to a strong central government.

Only one President has ever been from the Federalist Party: John Adams (1797–1801). He supported the interest of businesses and landowners, and wanted to keep close ties to the British monarchy.

Republican

The Republican party, also known as the Grand Old Party (GOP), is based on **conservative** views. The party believes in spending money on the army, limiting government support for programs such as nationwide healthcare, and reducing taxes for everyone. There have been a total of 18 Republican Presidents, starting with Abraham Lincoln.

William McKinley (President No. 25), 1897–1901.

Democratic

Today's Democratic party members have mainly **liberal** views toward helping the community, rather than focusing on individuals. Many Democrats believe that taxes for some people should be raised to fund government programs for everyone, and that there should be healthcare for all Americans.

Barack Obama (President No. 44), 2009–2017.

Whig

The Whig party felt that Congress should have more power than the President. Four Presidents were members of the Whig party. The Whigs didn't last very long because many Whigs fought over whether to allow slavery in the newly formed American territories. This resulted in the breakup of the party after President Millard Fillmore left the office in 1853.

Millard Fillmore (President No. 13), 1850–1853.

Independent

Presidents who do not choose one party over another, like George Washington, or are expelled from their party, like John Tyler (see page 42), are considered Independent. Zachary Taylor was an Independent who joined the Whigs when he ran for President.

Zachary Taylor (President No. 12), 1849–1850.

VICE PRESIDENTS AND THE CABINET

Vice Presidents (VPs)

Vice Presidents are second in command and will assume the role of the President if anything happens to the President. Vice Presidents also have the role as the president of the Senate, and they are allowed to vote on **bills** in the Senate when a tiebreak is needed. Vice Presidents were originally the presidential candidates receiving the second-largest number of votes. Now, presidential candidates choose their own running mate and a vote for one is automatically a vote for the other.

Barack Obama and Vice President Joe Biden.

From Vice President to President

Fourteen Presidents served first as Vice Presidents. Many of them, such as John Tyler (President No. 10), Theodore Roosevelt (President No. 26), and Lyndon B. Johnson (President No. 36), took over the presidency when the President in office died suddenly from illness, or was **assassinated**.

John Adams (President No. 2) was America's first Vice President.

The Cabinet

The President's **cabinet** are people who are hired to assist the President. The tradition of the cabinet was created in the Constitution and dates back to George Washington, who appointed a cabinet of four people: Secretary of State Thomas Jefferson; Secretary of the Treasury Alexander Hamilton; Secretary of War Henry Knox; and Attorney General Edmund Randolph. Today, the cabinet is made up of advisers in many different areas, including Education, Agriculture, and Justice. There are 15 different departments to help with anything the President needs.

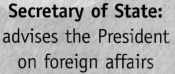

Secretary of State: advises the President on foreign affairs

Attorney General: advises the President about the law and legal affairs

President

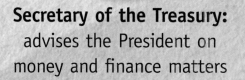

Secretary of the Treasury: advises the President on money and finance matters

Secretary of Defense: advises the President on matters relating to war and the military

U.S. PRESIDENTS
AND VICE PRESIDENTS

George Washington

1 1789–1797
VP: John Adams

John Adams

2 1797–1801
VP: Thomas Jefferson

Thomas Jefferson

3 1801–1809
VP: Aaron Burr/
George Clinton

James Madison

4 1809–1817
VP: George Clinton/
Elbridge Gerry

James Monroe

5 1817–1825
VP: Daniel D. Tompkins

John Quincy Adams

6 1825–1829
VP: John C. Calhoun

Andrew Jackson

7 1829–1837
VP: John C. Calhoun/
Martin Van Buren

Martin Van Buren

8 1837–1841
VP: Richard M. Johnson

William Henry Harrison

9 1841–1841
VP: John Tyler

John Tyler

10 1841–1845
VP: none

James Polk

11 1845–1849
VP: George M. Dallas

Zachary Taylor

12 1849–1850
VP: Millard Fillmore

Millard Fillmore

13 1850–1853
VP: none

Franklin Pierce

14 1853–1857
VP: William R. King

James Buchanan

15 1857–1861
VP: John C. Breckinridge

Abraham Lincoln

16 1861–1865
VP: Hannibal Hamlin/
Andrew Johnson

Andrew Johnson

17 1865–1869
VP: none

Ulysses S. Grant

18 1869–1877
VP: Schuyler Colfax/
Henry Wilson

Rutherford B. Hayes

19 1877–1881
VP: William A. Wheeler

James Garfield

20 1881–1881
VP: Chester A. Arthur

Chester A. Arthur

21 1881–1885
VP: none

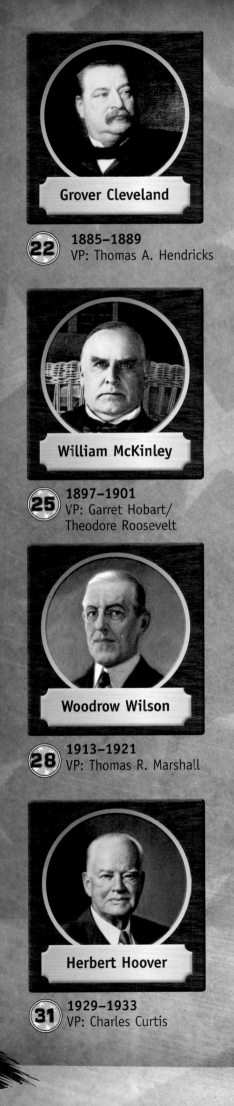

Grover Cleveland

22 1885–1889
VP: Thomas A. Hendricks

Benjamin Harrison

23 1889–1893
VP: Levi P. Morton

Grover Cleveland

24 1893–1897
VP: Adlai Stevenson

William McKinley

25 1897–1901
VP: Garret Hobart/
Theodore Roosevelt

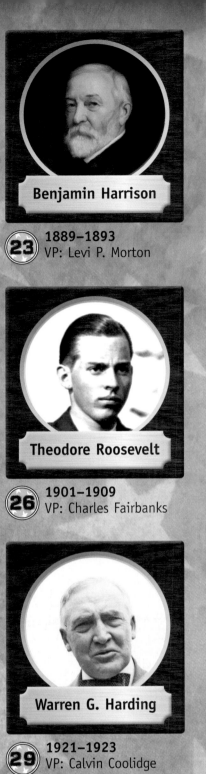

Theodore Roosevelt

26 1901–1909
VP: Charles Fairbanks

William Howard Taft

27 1909–1913
VP: James S. Sherman

Woodrow Wilson

28 1913–1921
VP: Thomas R. Marshall

Warren G. Harding

29 1921–1923
VP: Calvin Coolidge

Calvin Coolidge

30 1923–1929
VP: Charles G. Dawes

Herbert Hoover

31 1929–1933
VP: Charles Curtis

Franklin D. Roosevelt

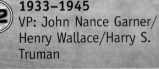

32 1933–1945
VP: John Nance Garner/
Henry Wallace/Harry S.
Truman

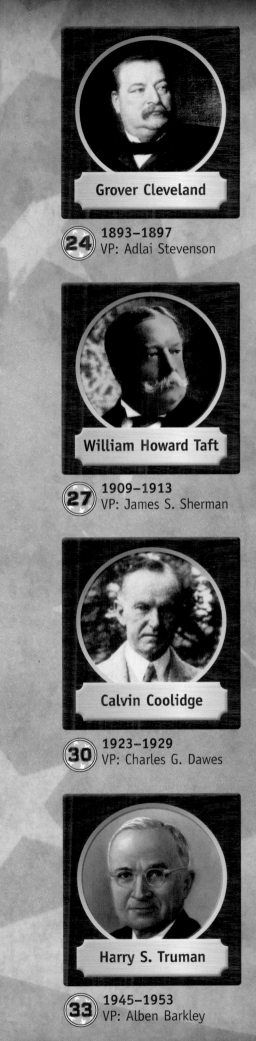

Harry S. Truman

33 1945–1953
VP: Alben Barkley

Dwight D. Eisenhower

34 1953–1961
VP: Richard Nixon

John F. Kennedy

35 1961–1963
VP: Lyndon B. Johnson

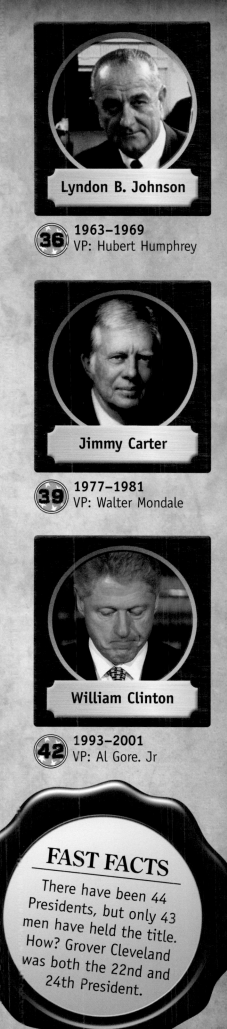

Lyndon B. Johnson

36 1963–1969
VP: Hubert Humphrey

Richard M. Nixon

37 1969–1974
VP: Spiro Agnew/
Gerald Ford

Gerald Ford

38 1974–1977
VP: Nelson Rockefeller

Jimmy Carter

39 1977–1981
VP: Walter Mondale

Ronald Reagan

40 1981–1989
VP: George H.W. Bush

George H. W. Bush

41 1989–1993
VP: Dan Quayle

William Clinton

42 1993–2001
VP: Al Gore. Jr

George W. Bush

43 2001–2009
VP: Dick Cheney

Barack Obama

44 2009–2017
VP: Joe Biden

FAST FACTS

There have been 44 Presidents, but only 43 men have held the title. How? Grover Cleveland was both the 22nd and 24th President.

THE 1700S

For the United States of America, the 1700s was the era when it all began. But what else was going on at this time?

1732 George Washington is born.

1700 — 1710 — 1720 — 1730 — 1740

1702–1713 Queen Anne's War, in which France loses North American territory to Britain, is fought.

1721 One of many smallpox epidemics breaks out in New England, leading to a push for vaccination.

1734 Famous explorer Daniel Boone is born. Boone discovered trading routes and founded towns all the way to what is now Kentucky.

1716 The first theater in the colonies opens in Williamsburg, Virginia.

1717 The Conestoga Wagon is invented, and is used to transport heavy loads to the lands beyond the 13 colonies.

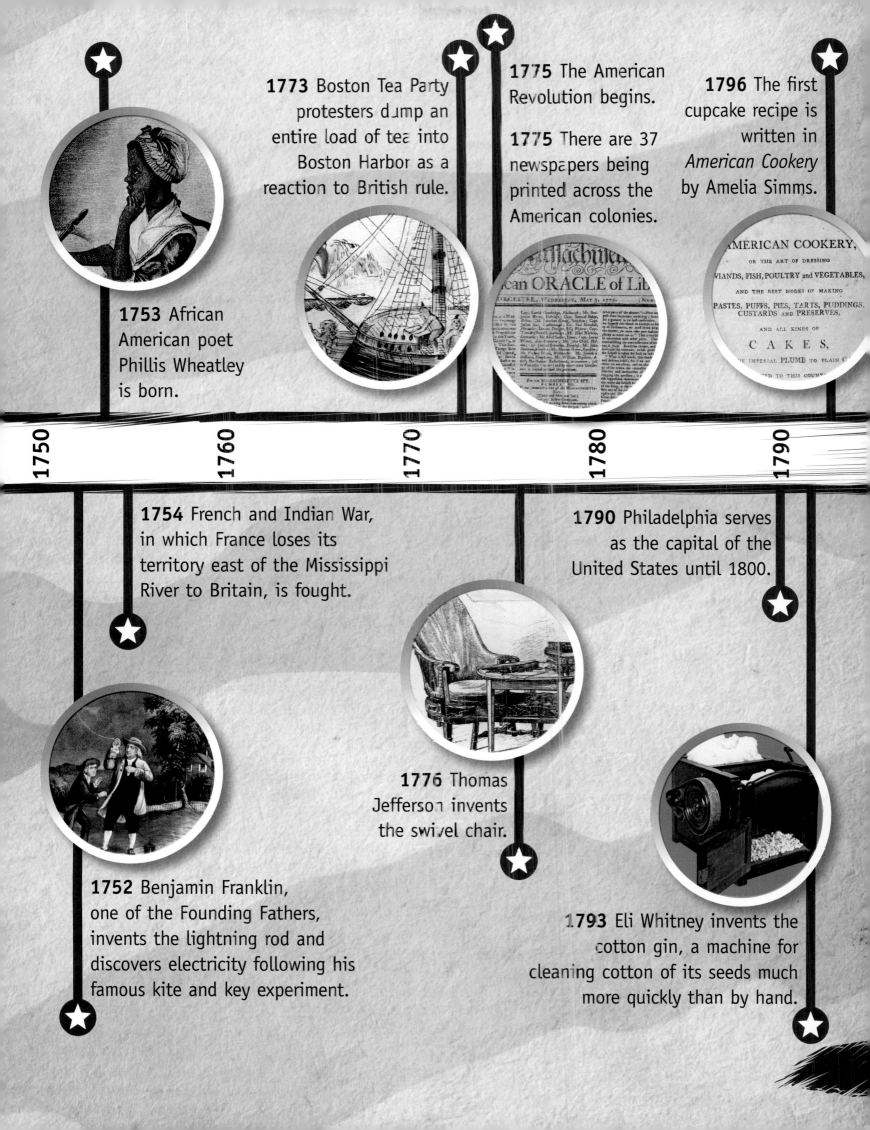

1773 Boston Tea Party protesters dump an entire load of tea into Boston Harbor as a reaction to British rule.

1775 The American Revolution begins.

1775 There are 37 newspapers being printed across the American colonies.

1796 The first cupcake recipe is written in *American Cookery* by Amelia Simms.

1753 African American poet Phillis Wheatley is born.

AMERICAN COOKERY,
OR THE ART OF DRESSING
VIANDS, FISH, POULTRY and VEGETABLES,
AND THE BEST MODES OF MAKING
PASTES, PUFFS, PIES, TARTS, PUDDINGS,
CUSTARDS AND PRESERVES,
AND ALL KINDS OF
CAKES,

1750 1760 1770 1780 1790

1754 French and Indian War, in which France loses its territory east of the Mississippi River to Britain, is fought.

1790 Philadelphia serves as the capital of the United States until 1800.

1776 Thomas Jefferson invents the swivel chair.

1752 Benjamin Franklin, one of the Founding Fathers, invents the lightning rod and discovers electricity following his famous kite and key experiment.

1793 Eli Whitney invents the cotton gin, a machine for cleaning cotton of its seeds much more quickly than by hand.

1. GEORGE WASHINGTON

George Washington was a commander who led the colonists and won the fight against the British during the American Revolution (1775–83). He helped to write the U.S. Constitution, creating the laws of the new nation. In 1789, he became the first President of the United States.

The British, under the leadership of General Charles Cornwallis (front right), surrendered to General George Washington (front left) at the Battle of Yorktown on October 19, 1781.

FAST FACTS

Lived from: 1732–1799
Years in office: 1789–1797
Party: None
Vice President (VP): John Adams

Money, Money, Money

It is thought that by the time of his death, Washington was the wealthiest American of his era. But when he first became President, he was often short on cash! He refused his salary of $25,000 per year because he thought it set a bad example for future presidents. (In the end, he accepted it to pay for living expenses.)

LIBERTY
IN GOD WE TRUST
1984

Today we see George Washington's face on the quarter and the $1 bill

This pair of Washington's dentures can still be seen at his home in Mount Vernon, NY.

It's a Myth...

...that George Washington had wooden teeth, but he did have terrible chompers. He only had one of his own teeth left by the time he became President. The dentures he wore may have looked like wood, but they were actually made out of everything from bone, brass springs, lead, gold, and even other human teeth!

ONE AND ONLY!

George Washington was the only President to be elected unanimously (with the agreement of everyone)—and he did it twice. He received all the votes in 1789, and again in 1792.

Father of His Country

George Washington served two **terms** as President. His first four years were largely spent organizing his cabinet and creating the rules and procedures that would allow the government to run smoothly. During his second term, he kept the United States out of war with Europe, and spent his efforts on strengthening the new nation.

George Washington reads out the oath of office at his inauguration.

The New President

Washington's first **inauguration** took place at the Federal Hall, New York, in 1789. At his second inauguration in 1793, Washington made the shortest inaugural speech on record—133 words. It lasted for less than two minutes.

At his first inauguration, Washington stood on the Federal Hall balcony before a crowd of 10,000 people.

A New Capital

Initially, representatives from each state met in New York, Philadelphia, and other cities until a permanent capital could be found. In 1790, Washington chose a ten mile by ten mile site to form the new capital. A year later, the new, unbuilt city was named Washington in his honor.

In 1790, the city of Washington didn't yet exist. It was founded in 1791 on the Potomac River.

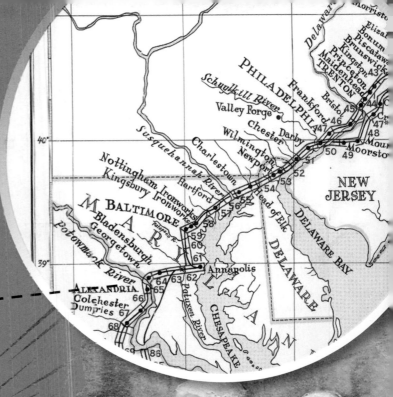

KEY EVENTS

- **September 1787** The Constitution is signed.

- **1787–1789** The first states **ratify** the Constitution.

- **April 1789** Washington is elected the first President of the United States.

- **September 1796** Washington writes his Farewell Address to the nation at the end of his second term as President.

2. JOHN ADAMS

John Adams served as Vice President under George Washington for eight years before being elected President in 1797. Known as the "Father of the American Navy," Adams felt the country needed a strong naval force to compete against France and Britain, who were at war with each other. In 1798, Adams signed an unpopular law allowing the government to arrest and deport (send home) immigrants. As a result, he lost the reelection to Thomas Jefferson in 1801.

Adams liked hunting and fishing so much as a child that he often skipped school!

Wet Paint!

Adams was the first President to live in the newly built President's house, which later became known as the White House, in Washington, D.C. He lived there for four months in 1800, while the paint was still wet! On the day Adams and his family moved to the President's house, they got lost in the woods nearby before finding their way there.

The President's house wasn't named the "White House" until Theodore Roosevelt moved in, 100 years later.

Adams and Jefferson

Adams and Thomas Jefferson were two of the Founding Fathers of the United States, and together they drafted the Declaration of Independence. They didn't agree on many issues—including how much power the new government should have—but wound up becoming fast friends. They even died on the same day—July 4, 1826—exactly 50 years after the Declaration of Independence was signed!

John Adams (center), Thomas Jefferson (right), and Benjamin Franklin (left) review a draft of the Declaration of Independence.

Adams ordered a fleet of battleships to be built, including the frigate *U.S.S. Constitution*, launched in 1797.

THAT'S A FIRST!

In 1798, Adams created the United States Marine Band, the oldest professional musical organization in the country. He also created a new position in his cabinet for a Secretary of the Navy.

THE 1800S

The new United States has made it through its early years—full of battles and stumbles, but is well on its way to becoming a great nation.

1844 Samuel Morse sends the first telegraph from the U.S. Capitol in Washington, D.C. to Baltimore.

1800	1810	1820	1830	1840

1814 The British burn Washington, D.C. and the White House.

1830 The first steam locomotive in the United States is built—the Baltimore and Ohio Railroad's train, *Tom Thumb*.

1820 James Monroe (President No. 5) creates the Monroe Doctrine, stating that the United States was closed to future colonization.

1846–1848 The Mexican American War is fought, brought on by the United States' **annexation** of Texas.

1812–1815 The final war with Britain, the War of 1812, ends in a stalemate— neither side loses territory.

1830s The **Underground Railroad** is established— a network of safehouses used by slaves to escape to free states and Canada.

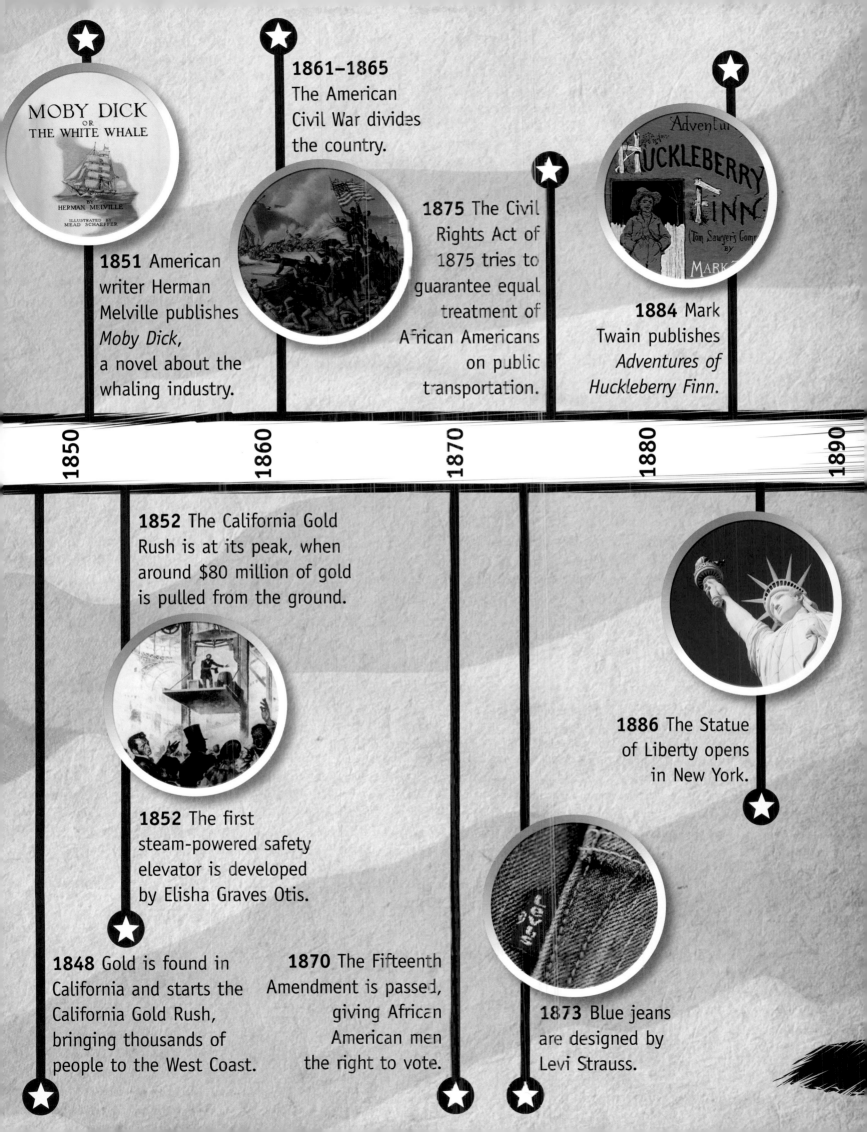

1851 American writer Herman Melville publishes *Moby Dick*, a novel about the whaling industry.

1861–1865 The American Civil War divides the country.

1875 The Civil Rights Act of 1875 tries to guarantee equal treatment of African Americans on public transportation.

1884 Mark Twain publishes *Adventures of Huckleberry Finn.*

1850   1860   1870   1880   1890

1852 The California Gold Rush is at its peak, when around $80 million of gold is pulled from the ground.

1852 The first steam-powered safety elevator is developed by Elisha Graves Otis.

1886 The Statue of Liberty opens in New York.

1848 Gold is found in California and starts the California Gold Rush, bringing thousands of people to the West Coast.

1870 The Fifteenth Amendment is passed, giving African American men the right to vote.

1873 Blue jeans are designed by Levi Strauss.

3. THOMAS JEFFERSON

FAST FACTS

Lived from: 1743–1826
Years in office: 1801–1809
Party: Democratic-Republican
VP: Aaron Burr/ George Clinton

When it comes to liberty, Thomas Jefferson wrote the book on it—or the declaration at least. The principal author of the Declaration of Independence, Jefferson thought that each state should have the ability to govern its citizens without too much intrusion from the federal government. He felt it was necessary for the President to stick to the rules exactly as they were laid out in the Constitution. Despite being a shy man in office, Jefferson proved to be a powerful and influential leader.

Jefferson presents the first draft of the Declaration of Independence in 1776.

Jefferson was a keen reader. His personal library had more than 6,700 books.

Louisiana Territory

In 1803, after he became the third President, Jefferson bought the Louisiana Territory from France. The territory wasn't just modern-day Louisiana—it included the entire middle of the country, all the way up to Montana. The purchase doubled the size of the United States!

The United States paid $15 million for the Louisiana Territory in 1803. That would be $240 million today.

Go West!

Jefferson commissioned the famous Lewis and Clark Expedition (1804–1806) to explore the new territory gained in the Louisiana Purchase, study the plant and animal life there, and create maps of America's Western frontier. Meriwether Lewis and William Clark spent two years trekking across the nation, making contact with the American Indian tribes, crossing the **Continental Divide**, viewing the Pacific, and mapping their journey.

Without help from American Indians, the members of the Lewis and Clark Expedition would have starved.

THAT'S A FIRST!

Jefferson was the first President to have his inauguration in the new capital, Washington, D.C. (George Washington was inaugurated in New York and Philadelphia, and John Adams in Philadelphia as well!)

Interests and Education

Jefferson designed his own house, called Monticello, and filled it with many unique features, including skylights and octagonal rooms. There he pursued a huge range of interests, from scientific experiments to philosophy. Jefferson also thought education was really important. He created the University of Virginia, which was founded on land that belonged to James Monroe (President No. 5)!

Jefferson built his Virginia home, Monticello, and used it for his many scientific pursuits.

Rest in Peace

On his tombstone, Jefferson wanted it carved that he was the author of the Declaration of Independence, but didn't add that he was also the President of the United States!

HERE WAS BURIED
THOMAS JEFFERSON
AUTHOR OF THE
DECLARATION
OF
AMERICAN INDEPENDENCE
OF THE
STATUTE OF VIRGINIA
FOR
RELIGIOUS FREEDOM
AND FATHER OF THE
UNIVERSITY OF VIRGINIA

Jefferson wanted his tomb to be made of coarse stone rather than marble so that no one would want to steal it for its value.

A Plant Family

Jefferson had a family of plants named after him by the botanist Benjamin Smith Barton, who lived in the late eighteenth century. The Latin name for the plants is *Jeffersonia diphylla*.

The Jeffersonia diphylla, or twinleaf.

Another Family

Jefferson was against slavery, yet he owned more than 600 slaves during his lifetime. One of his slaves was Sally Hemings (ca. 1773–1885), who is thought to have been Jefferson's mistress for 38 years, and may have had children with him.

KEY EVENTS

- **March 1801** Jefferson becomes the 3rd President.
- **April 1803** Jefferson signs the Louisiana Purchase treaty.
- **August 1803** Lewis begins his expedition. Clark joins the following year.

Jefferson's slaves greet the President as he arrives back home from a trip abroad.

4. JAMES MADISON

FAST FACTS

Lived from: 1751–1836
Years in office: 1809–1817
Party: Democratic-Republican
VP: George Clinton/
Elbridge Gerry

James Madison is known as the "Father of the Constitution." He was a member of the Constitutional Convention, a group of men who came up with the format for the new U.S. government. He also co-wrote The Federalist Papers— letters convincing his fellow Americans to ratify the Constitution—and he also helped shape the Bill of Rights.

Madison was one of two Presidents to sign the Constitution. (Washington was the other.)

War of 1812

Madison reacted to Britain's attacks on American ships at sea by telling Americans not to trade with Britain. When that didn't work, he declared war. During the War of 1812, the British marched into Washington, D.C. and set fire to the White House and the Capitol (the building where Congress meets). But by 1815, America had defended itself and ended the war.

The White House and U.S. Capitol were burned by the British in 1812.

America defeated the British in the Battle of Orleans, 1815, the final major battle of the War of 1812.

First Lady

The first official inaugural ball occurred in 1809. Madison was sworn in as President at the U.S. Capitol, and that evening his wife, Dolley Madison, hosted a dance at the White House. She sold 400 tickets, at $4 per ticket (that would be $60 today).

Dolley Madison was the first to be called the "First Lady," a term used by Zachary Taylor at her state funeral in 1849.

THAT'S A FIRST!

Madison was the first President not to wear a wig on top of his own hair in public. He was also the first President to wear long pants instead of knee breeches!

5. JAMES MONROE

FAST FACTS

Lived from: 1758–1831
Years in office: 1817–1825
Party: Democratic-Republicans
VP: Daniel D. Tompkins

James Monroe wanted his presidency to be remembered as an "era of good feelings." But when the people of the Missouri territory wanted to become a new state, a bitter struggle began. States in the North wanted it to be a free state (one that did not allow slavery), whereas states in the South wanted it to be a slave state (one that allows it).

Monrovia, the capital of Liberia in Africa, is named for Monroe.

The Missouri Compromise

In 1820, a compromise was agreed. Missouri would join the United States as a slave state, but Maine, which also wanted to join the United States, would be a free state. This was known as the Missouri Compromise. It also outlawed slavery north of the lands bought in the Louisiana Purchase of 1803.

This map from 1820 shows the free states (shaded in yellow), including Maine, and the slave states (in brown), including Missouri.

Hands Off!

Monroe wanted to make sure that the portions of America not part of the **Union** (especially the Pacific coast and parts of Latin America) would not be colonized by foreigners, especially people from Europe and Russia. He created a **policy** that would become known as the Monroe Doctrine: "the American continents . . . are henceforth not to be considered as subjects for future colonization by any European Power."

In this cartoon, Uncle Sam (the United States) is caging in the roosters (European countries) to stop them from colonizing his territory.

Monroe with his officials creating the Monroe Doctrine in 1823.

NEARLY PERFECT

In his reelection, Monroe won all the votes but one. Rumor had it that Senator William Plumer voted against him to preserve the legacy of Washington, the only President elected unanimously. Plumer said he just didn't like Monroe.

6. JOHN QUINCY ADAMS

Quincy Adams
was fluent in
seven languages.

FAST FACTS

Lived from: 1767–1848
Years in office: 1825–1829
Party: Democratic Republicans
VP: John C. Calhoun

During the 1824 presidential election, neither John Quincy Adams nor the military general Andrew Jackson won the majority of votes needed to become President. The election was decided by the **House of Representatives**, and Quincy Adams won. Quincy Adams proposed many new laws to improve society—such as constructing roads, canals, and universities—but few were carried out. In his later years, he supported freedom of speech and opposed slavery.

Taking a Dip

Quincy Adams liked to go skinny dipping in the Potomac River. One reporter, Ann Royall, once stole his clothes and refused to give them back until he agreed to an interview. Quincy Adams had to say yes, so he was the first President to grant an interview to a female journalist.

The Potomac River forms the border between Washington, D.C. and Virginia.

Pretty as a Picture

Quincy Adams's portrait is the oldest surviving photograph of a President. He was not the first President to be photographed—William Henry Harrison (President No. 9) had a portrait taken at his inauguration in 1841, but that picture has been lost.

This photo of Quincy Adams dates back to the late 1840s.

Quincy Adams ordered the construction of the Erie Canal in 1825. It provided the first transportation from New York City to the Great Lakes by water.

7. ANDREW JACKSON

FAST FACTS

Lived from: 1767–1845
Years in office: 1829–1837
Party: Democratic
VP: Martin Van Buren

Andrew Jackson was a feisty war hero who became President. Jackson led a new Democratic party that supported the average man and the states, and slavery in the western territories. He was strong-willed and fiery, often using his powers of presidential **veto** to get what he wanted. Before he became President, it is said that he was involved in hundreds of duels and brawls. If you can believe it, he lived for 40 years with a bullet in his chest from a duel!

Jackson winning a pistol duel in the early 1800s.

Indian Removal Act

Jackson decided that if American Indian tribes wanted to keep their own form of government, they had to move outside of the existing states. In 1830, he introduced the Indian Removal Act that would transport the American Indians west of the Mississippi River. They resisted and had to be moved by force. The journey they made is known as the Trail of Tears.

Cherokee Indians were forced from their homelands during the 1830s on the Trail of Tears.

Andrew Jackson was a general during the War of 1812 against the British.

Now That's a Party!

After Jackson's first inaugural address in 1829, a crowd of people came to the President's house for a reception. The party got out of hand; china and glassware were smashed and President Jackson had to escape by leaving through a window.

Citizens going to the White House reception after Jackson's inauguration.

ONE AND ONLY!

Jackson was the only President to serve in both the American Revolution and the War of 1812, and to be a prisoner of war. He was captured by the British during the American Revolution.

9. WILLIAM HENRY HARRISON

William Henry Harrison was President for just 32 days, from March 4, 1841 to April 4, 1841. He gave the longest inauguration speech in history, lasting one hour and 40 minutes, speaking outside in bad weather without a coat or hat on. He died of pneumonia one month later!

William Henry Harrison was the grandfather of Benjamin Harrison (President No. 23).

FAST FACTS

Lived from: 1773–1841
Years in office: 1841–1841
Party: Whig
VP: John Tyler

Tippecanoe and Tecumseh

Before becoming President, Harrison was Governor of the Indiana Territory. His task was to "buy" land from American Indians for the white settlers, and defend the new settlements. One Shawnee Indian chieftain, Tecumseh, organized a fight against Harrison's army. A battle ensued at Tippecanoe Creek on November 7, 1811, giving Harrison his nickname "Tippecanoe" or "Old Tip."

Tecumseh was killed in battle in 1813 and the American Indians never regained their lands.

ONE AND ONLY!

Harrison is the only President who went to medical school. His father wanted him to be a doctor, but Harrison dropped out to pursue a career in the military instead.

The death of Harrison on April 4, 1841.

What to Do?

The Constitution didn't actually say that a Vice President would become President after the President's death. (An amendment was added in 1967 to say just this, but back in 1841, no one knew what to do.) Harrison died on April 4, and John Tyler was sworn in on April 6. April 5 must have been a very confusing day!

This illustration shows John Tyler receiving the news of Harrison's sudden death.

10. JOHN TYLER

John Tyler favored states' rights and felt that the Constitution should be followed word for word. He is most famous for the annexation of Texas. Texas had been a Spanish colony, then a part of Mexico, then an independent republic before it joined the United States. Mexico had said that it would declare war if the United States made Texas a state, so the Mexican-American War (1846–1848) began.

Tyler wanted to be a concert violinist, but he settled for President instead!

A Party of One

Tyler's story is one that involves many parties. He was originally a Democratic-Republican but ran as a Whig to become Vice President under Harrison. After Harrison's death, he rose to the Presidency, but his policies clashed with Whig leader Henry Clay and he was expelled from the Whig Party. Tyler spent the rest of his term as an Independent.

Texans raising their flag over the Alamo, declaring their desire to be a part of the United States.

Henry Clay, leader of the Whig Party, disagreed with many of Tyler's policies.

Sherwood Forest

Tyler named his plantation back home in Virginia "Sherwood Forest." Maybe he thought he was Robin Hood! His descendants (distant relatives) still own and live in his house near Williamsburg.

The Sherwood Forest plantation was the home of John Tyler after his presidency.

11. JAMES POLK

Under James Polk, the United States increased in size by more than a third. For the first time, it reached all the way to the Pacific Ocean. Texas and Florida had just become states, and when America won the Mexican-American War, it gained the territories of California and New Mexico as well. With more territory, however, came more arguments. The North and South started to quarrel over whether the new territories should allow slavery. These disagreements would simmer until the outbreak of the Civil War in 1861.

At the age of 49, Polk was the youngest man up to that point to be elected President.

Mission Accomplished!

Polk made four campaign promises and fulfilled all of them: to lower **tariffs**, acquire California and New Mexico, add the Oregon Territory, and retire from office after one term.

In 1848, Polk's addition of New Mexico and Oregon (both outlined in yellow on the left) further increased the size of the United States.

The American army (in blue uniform) defeated the Mexicans at the Battle of Cerro Gordo (1847) during the Mexican-American War.

No "Polking" Fun

Polk's wife, Sarah, worked as the President's secretary without getting paid for it. She banned dancing, card-playing, and hard liquor from the White House and refused to go to the theater or horse races. She was absolutely no fun. However, she did host the very first White House Thanksgiving!

Polk's wife, Sarah Childress, was known to be a serious, sensible woman.

THAT'S A FIRST!

News of Polk's nomination for President was the first to be reported by telegraph (a system of transmitting messages by wire). It was set up by Samuel Morse and went from Baltimore to Washington, D.C. in 1844.

12. ZACHARY TAYLOR

FAST FACTS

Lived from: 1784–1850
Years in office: 1849–1850
Party: Whig
VP: Millard Fillmore

When Zachary Taylor became President, relations between the North and South were still strained over whether the new states should be free or allow slavery. The South even threatened to **secede** from the Union. Taylor, a **nationalist**, wanted to keep the country together. He allowed California and other new states to draft their own constitutions. This meant they would likely be free states, which angered the South further.

Taylor brought his skills as a confident army general to the presidency in 1849.

California Gold Rush

On January 24, 1848, a nugget of gold was found in Coloma, California. News spread and thousands of gold seekers traveled to the West Coast. They were known as "forty-niners" because they journeyed to California during 1849. The influx of people meant that cities, businesses, and railroads quickly formed, grew, and expanded.

"Forty-niners" came to California in search of gold.

Major General Zachary Taylor was a hero in the Mexican-American War (1846–1848).

Cherries and Milk

Taylor died in office after only a year and a half as President. He was attending a ceremony on a hot day—July 4, 1850. He ate cherries and drank a glass of milk, then became sick and died five days later. Some believe the cause was bacteria from the cherries; others think he was poisoned. No poison was found in his body when it was reexamined in 1991, so the most likely culprit was contaminated food.

Taylor died after just 16 months as President.

13. MILLARD FILLMORE

FAST FACTS

Lived from: 1800–1874
Years in office: 1850–1853
Party: Whig
VP: None

Although Millard Fillmore was antislavery, it would be the infamous Compromise of 1850 for which people would remember him. In this set of laws, California would become a free state, Utah and New Mexico would decide for themselves whether to allow slavery, and the slave trade would be abolished in Washington, D.C. However, as part of the Compromise, the devastating Fugitive Slave Act was passed.

Fugitive Slave Act

The Fugitive Slave Act required runaway slaves to be returned to their slaveowners, and the law denied captured slaves the right to a fair trial. Thousands of African Americans tried to escape to Canada. The Underground Railroad became more active than ever.

This painting illustrates a kind farmer and his family leading a group of runaway slaves to freedom.

THAT'S A NO!

Fillmore was offered an honorary degree in Latin from Oxford University, but he didn't accept it. Why? "I had not the advantages of a classical education and I don't feel any man should accept a degree he cannot read."

A portrait of Fillmore painted in 1843.

Young Love

Fillmore only went to school for six months, but it would be an influential time in his life. He was 17 and fell in love with his 19-year-old teacher, Abigail Powers, whom he would marry several years later, in 1826.

Abigail, Fillmore's wife, shared her husband's passion for learning.

14. FRANKLIN PIERCE

FAST FACTS

Lived from: 1804–1869
Years in office: 1853–1857
Party: Democratic
VP: William R. King

Franklin Pierce, a Democrat from New Hampshire, tried to appeal to both the North and the South, but his ideas on expanding America's borders and adding territory angered many antislavery supporters. They feared that more states might mean more slave states.

"We 'Polked' you in 1844, we shall 'Pierce' you in 1852" was Pierce's presidential campaign slogan.

The Kansas-Nebraska Act

The United States was growing into a huge nation, one that would need railroads. The Kansas-Nebraska Act (1854) gained land for the railroads, but allowed Kansas and Nebraska to choose whether to be a free or slave state. Fierce fighting broke out in Kansas between antislavery and proslavery supporters. This violence would lead, eventually, to the Civil War in 1861.

Tensions ran high in Kansas in 1858 between supporters of slavery and those opposed.

The inauguration of Pierce as the fourteenth President of the United States, on March 4, 1853.

THAT'S A FIRST!

Every incoming President must either *swear* or *affirm* (declare) to defend the Constitution. There are two choices because some religions ask believers to not swear. Pierce (an Episcopalian) is the first and only President to *affirm* the oath.

Worst to First

During his second year at Bowdoin College, Maine, Pierce had the lowest grades in his class. Yet, as President, he was able to give his 20-minute inaugural speech from memory, without any notes. What a turnaround! Two of Pierce's classmates were Nathaniel Hawthorne and Henry Wadsworth Longfellow, men who would go on to become important writers.

Born the same year as Pierce, author Nathaniel Hawthorne (1804–1864) went on to write The Scarlet Letter.

15. JAMES BUCHANAN

The debates over slavery that had been boiling for the past decade were getting worse. James Buchanan thought it was a matter for the states to decide. He interfered as little as possible but, in the end, this didn't work. Buchanan is, sadly, remembered for not being able to halt the tensions that would lead to the Civil War.

FAST FACTS

Lived from: 1791–1868
Years in office: 1857–1861
Party: Democratic
VP: John C. Breckinridge

Buchanan is the only President who comes from Pennsylvania.

ONE AND ONLY!

Buchanan was the only President never to marry. He may have been the first gay President. Letters he wrote suggest that he had great affection for William R. King, the former Vice President.

Dred Scott

In 1857, an African American slave named Dred Scott moved with his owner from a slave state to a free state. Scott tried to **sue** his owner for his freedom. But the Supreme Court made its notorious "Dred Scott" decision: The federal government would have no power to stop slavery in any of its territories, and any African Americans would be denied the rights of U.S. citizenship. In essence, a slave, such as Scott, could not claim freedom—no matter where he lived. This caused outrage and deepened the North-South divide, leading to the Civil War.

Buchanan wanted to keep the peace between proslavery and antislavery supporters.

Dred Scott was an African American slave who tried, but failed, to gain his freedom.

Harpers Ferry

In October 1859, John Brown, a white **abolitionist**, tried to create a slave revolt by raiding the federal arsenal (a building that contained weapons) at Harpers Ferry, Virginia. Brown and his men failed and he was convicted of treason and hanged. This violence added to the distrust between proslavery and antislavery leaders, which would culminate in the Civil War.

John Brown and his men raiding the Harpers Ferry armory in 1859.

The Gettysburg Address

In 1863, Lincoln made the Gettysburg Address—a famous speech that starts: "Four score and seven years ago our fathers brought forth on this continent a new nation, conceived in liberty, and dedicated to the proposition that all men are created equal." The speech memorialized the men who fought at the Battle of Gettysburg during the Civil War. More importantly, it reminded the nation of the purpose of the war and supported human equality.

When Lincoln delivered the Gettysburg Address, he was suffering from smallpox!

The Thirteenth Amendment

Lincoln knew that the Emancipation Proclamation of 1863 was not part of the Constitution, so it might not be followed after the war. So he added a law to the Constitution to state: "neither slavery nor involuntary servitude ... shall exist within the United States." The Thirteenth Amendment passed on December 18, 1865.

The House of Representatives celebrating the passing of the Thirteenth Amendment in 1863.

Ford's Theater

On April 14, 1865, President Lincoln went to the theater to see the play *Our American Cousin*. During the show, a man named John Wilkes Booth, a former actor who was strongly opposed to the abolition of slavery, shot the President, leapt off the balcony, and escaped. The President died the next day. The manhunt for Booth lasted 12 days. He was tracked down in Virginia and was shot before he could go to trial for his crime.

Booth shot Lincoln on Good Friday. Lincoln died nine hours later in a house across the street from the theater.

KEY EVENTS

- **March 1861** Lincoln is inaugurated.
- **April 1861** The American Civil War begins.
- **January 1863** Lincoln announces the Emancipation Proclamation and frees slaves.
- **July 1863** The Battle of Gettysburg.
- **March 1865** Lincoln is inaugurated for a second term.
- **April 1865** Lincoln is assassinated.

17. ANDREW JOHNSON

FAST FACTS

Lived from: 1808–1875
Years in office: 1865–1869
Party: Democratic/Independent
VP: None

Andrew Johnson was a Congressman from Tennessee during the Civil War. He was the only senator from the South to remain loyal to the Union, making him a hero to the North and a traitor to the South. His loyalty gained him the Presidency in 1865. Johnson spent the years after the Civil War restoring the Southern states to the Union. In 1868, he was the first President to be **impeached.**

Johnson was a poor tailor from the South who rose through the ranks to become President.

Not Above the Law

The impeachment trial of Johnson took place before the Senate in 1868. Congress said he illegally fired one of his staff. He was tried and acquitted (found not guilty) by one vote. It would be another 130 years before another president, Bill Clinton (President No. 42), would be impeached.

THAT'S A FIRST!

Johnson was the first President to host a baseball team at the White House, with the Washington Nationals and the Brooklyn Athletics, in 1865. He was also the first to call baseball "our national game."

The Fourteenth Amendment

The Fourteenth Amendment was passed by Congress in 1866 and ratified by the states in 1868, even without the President's support. It gave citizenship to all born in the United States, including former African American slaves.

Citizens cheering at the passing of the Fourteenth Amendment.

18. ULYSSES S. GRANT

A commander of the Union Army and a victorious hero during the Civil War, Grant easily won the election for President at the age of 46. His time in office was part of the **Reconstruction** era, in which the states that had broken away to form the Confederacy were brought back into the Union.

Grant was a successful general of the Union Army during the Civil War.

Fifteenth Amendment

The third and last Amendment of the Reconstruction period was the Fifteenth Amendment, which was adopted on March 30, 1870, during Grant's presidency. This law made it illegal to withhold male citizens' right to vote based on race, color, or whether they were previously enslaved.

The Fifteenth Amendment granted African American men the right to vote.

In Favor of Change

Grant was the first President to host an American Indian Chief in the White House. He was in favor of changing the treatment given to American Indians. His policies attempted to move them onto reservations and help them become farmers, but the government failed to support these policies and little changed.

Grant's body was laid to rest in a huge tomb, called a mausoleum. It is the largest in North America.

American Indian chiefs visiting Grant in the White House, 1871

THAT'S A FIRST!

Grant was the first President to run against a woman candidate, Virginia Woodhull, the nominee of the "Equal Rights Party" in 1872. Woodhull was a pioneer of women's rights at a time before women were even allowed to vote.

20. JAMES GARFIELD

In 1881, Garfield had just settled into his new position as President and begun the tasks that he planned to accomplish when, only 100 days into his first term, he was shot.

Garfield had originally wanted to be a sailor, but he became a teacher of Greek and Latin, and then a minister, before entering politics.

FAST FACTS

Lived from: 1831–1881
Years in office: 1881–1881
Party: Republican
VP: Chester A. Arthur

Who Shot Garfield?

Charles Guiteau, a lawyer from Illinois, shot Garfield with a five-barrel, 44-caliber revolver called a British Bulldog. He was angry that Garfield had not chosen him to serve in the government. Guiteau said he chose the ivory-handled gun because it would look good in a museum. The gun has since been lost.

In 1882, Charles Guiteau was convicted and hanged for assassinating the President.

Death of a President

Although Garfield's bullet wound was not life-threatening at first, doctors were unable to find the bullet. After three months of agony, Garfield, age 49, died from a blood infection and internal bleeding. Even inventor Alexander Graham Bell tried and failed to find the bullet with a metal detector he designed.

THAT'S A FIRST!

Garfield was the first ambidextrous President (he could write with his left and right hands). He also knew Latin and Greek, and would impress people by writing in Latin with one hand and in Greek with the other hand at the same time!

Alexander Graham Bell and his assistant use an electrical detector to find a bullet in Garfield's body, in 1881.

22. GROVER CLEVELAND

FAST FACTS

Lived from: 1837–1908
Years in office: 1885–1889
Party: Democratic
VP: Thomas A. Hendricks

Grover Cleveland is the only President to leave the White House and then return to it as President four years later (see him again on page 74). In the first of Cleveland's two terms in office, he tried to reduce the amount of money spent by the government. He would go on to lose the election in 1888, but run and win again in 1892.

Cleveland vetoed 414 bills during his presidency, twice as many as all 21 of the Presidents who came before him, combined.

Lady Liberty

Cleveland dedicated the Statue of Liberty on October 28, 1886. The statue was a gift from France to thank America for its alliance (friendship) during the French Revolution (1789–1799). The copper statue is 151 feet tall and arrived by boat in 350 different pieces. It was originally meant to work as a lighthouse!

The front cover of a French newspaper from 1886 shows the assembly of the Statue of Liberty in New York Harbor.

THAT'S A FIRST!

Grover Cleveland passed the New York exam to become a lawyer on his first try even though he never attended college or law school. Then, as a sheriff in New York in 1871–74, he was required to be the town hangman as well!

New York City celebrates the unveiling of the Statue of Liberty in 1886.

White House Wedding

Grover Cleveland is the only President to be married in a ceremony held at the White House. He married Frances Folsom in the Blue Room on June 2, 1886. Slices of Cleveland's wedding cake still exist. It was fruitcake and he gave out slices in satin boxes as wedding souvenirs.

Cleveland's wedding took place in the White House Blue Room in 1886.

24. GROVER CLEVELAND

FAST FACTS

Lived from: 1837–1908
Years in office: 1893–1897
Party: Democratic
VP: Adlai Stevenson

The country was having a terrible time when Grover Cleveland took office for the second time. Eighteen percent of American workers had no job, banks were closing, construction of new railroads had slowed by 50 percent, and charities didn't have the money to help all the people in need. The "Panic of 1893," as it was known, lasted for most of Cleveland's second term as President.

The New York Stock Exchange during the Panic of 1893, when stock prices fell and 500 banks closed.

No Solution

Cleveland didn't believe that it was the government's job to create work for the **unemployed** and he used the Army to forcefully resolve disagreements between workers and their bosses. Cleveland became unpopular with his party and with the public, and he decided not to try to run for President again.

A freight train was wrecked during the Pullman Strike of 1894, when railroad workers protested because they weren't being paid.

Cleveland at his desk in the White House.

Gold or Silver?

During Cleveland's presidency, paper money could be exchanged for gold or silver. But many European countries and American businessmen didn't want to use silver as money, only gold, which was more valuable. Cleveland agreed to use only gold, believing that this would help the nation's economy. But, in a country that produced a lot of silver, this made him very unpopular. His idea had failed, and America sank deeper into financial **depression**.

Gold, not silver, was favored by Cleveland and wealthy Americans.

LIBERTY

1894

ONE AND ONLY!

Cleveland is the only President to have a child born while he was at the White House—his daughter, Esther, in 1893.

25. WILLIAM McKINLEY

FAST FACTS

Lived from: 1843–1901
Years in office: 1897–1901
Party: Republican
VP: Garret Hobart/ Theodore Roosevelt

William McKinley increased America's position as a world leader. He led the nation to victory in the Spanish-American War of 1898—a three-month war to free Cuba from Spanish rule. He also annexed the Hawaiian Islands and sent troops to China to help end the Boxer Rebellion (when Chinese nationalists had begun killing foreigners and Chinese Christians). Six months after his reelection, McKinley was shot; the third President to be assassinated in office. (The first two were Abraham Lincoln in 1865 and James Garfield in 1881.)

The assassination of McKinley in 1901.

The Good Luck Flower

McKinley often wore a red carnation on his lapel as a good luck charm. Supposedly, while shaking hands with a line of people after giving a speech in 1901, he gave the flower to a little girl. Seconds later, he was shot twice in the chest by a man who thought of the President as an enemy of the people. McKinley died eight days later.

McKinley pictured with the flower he always wore in his lapel.

American soldiers fighting the Spanish for Cuba's independence in the Spanish-American War of 1898.

First Ride

McKinley was the first President to ride in a steam-powered automobile—a Stanley Steamer—in 1899. He also rode in an electric automobile—the ambulance that took him to the hospital after he had been shot in 1901.

The automobile ambulance that drove McKinley to the hospital after his assassination.

AMBULANCE.

THE 1900S

The 1900s, or the 20th century, was the century when America became a dominant leader in world affairs.

1905 Einstein publishes his Theory of Relativity.

| 1900 | 1910 | 1920 | 1930 | 1940 |

1902 One of the first moving pictures (or movies) is made: *A Trip to the Moon*

1928 Walt Disney creates Mickey Mouse.

1939–1945 World War II starts in Europe. The USA joins the War in 1941.

1900 Horseless carriages, or cars, take to the streets. (Traffic lights didn't exist until 1923.)

1914–1918 World War I begins, following the assassination of Austrian Archduke Franz Ferdinand.

1929 The Wall Street Crash and the start of the **Great Depression**.

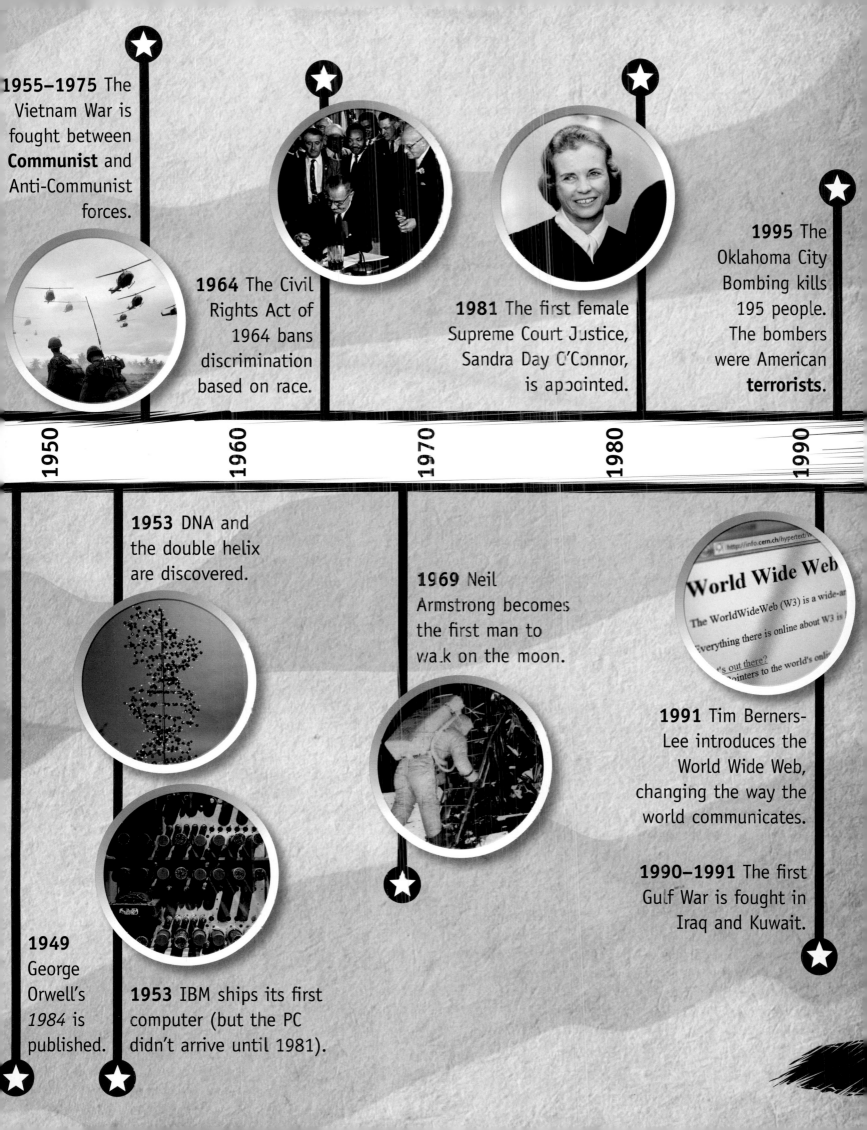

1955–1975 The Vietnam War is fought between **Communist** and Anti-Communist forces.

1964 The Civil Rights Act of 1964 bans discrimination based on race.

1981 The first female Supreme Court Justice, Sandra Day O'Connor, is appointed.

1995 The Oklahoma City Bombing kills 195 people. The bombers were American **terrorists**.

1950 1960 1970 1980 1990

1953 DNA and the double helix are discovered.

1969 Neil Armstrong becomes the first man to walk on the moon.

http://info.cern.ch/hypertext/W

World Wide Web

The WorldWideWeb (W3) is a wide-ar
Everything there is online about W3 is
's out there?
inters to the world's onli

1991 Tim Berners-Lee introduces the World Wide Web, changing the way the world communicates.

1990–1991 The first Gulf War is fought in Iraq and Kuwait.

1949 George Orwell's *1984* is published.

1953 IBM ships its first computer (but the PC didn't arrive until 1981).

26. THEODORE ROOSEVELT

FAST FACTS

Lived from: 1858–1919
Years in office: 1901–1909
Party: Republican
VP: Charles Fairbanks

Theodore "Teddy" Roosevelt was a man of many talents. He was a boxer, a cattle driver, the governor of New York, and a lieutenant colonel of the Rough Riders cavalry regiment during the Spanish-American War. As President, he used his power to attempt to improve the lives of American citizens, as well as establish peace abroad. He reformed overcrowded, poor working conditions, preserved the nation's wilderness, and kept businesses from becoming too large.

Teddy, an asthmatic when he was young, was encouraged by his father to take up horseback riding, boxing, and other forms of exercise to keep him healthy.

The Teddy Bear

Did you know that teddy bears got their name from "Teddy" Roosevelt? During a hunting trip in Mississippi in 1902, Roosevelt refused to shoot an injured bear. A shopkeeper heard about the incident and wrote to Roosevelt asking him permission to use his name "Teddy" for the stuffed toy bears he sold.

Teddy's bears became popular in 1902.

The Rough Riders cavalry with Colonel Roosevelt (center left) in 1898.

The Panama Canal

One of Roosevelt's most admired achievements was to establish the Panama Canal, building a passage between the Atlantic and Pacific Oceans through Central America (so boats didn't need to travel all the way around the southern tip of South America).

Container ships still carry goods through the Panama Canal in Central America rather than travel all the way around South America.

Environmental Legacy

Throughout his travels, Roosevelt became alarmed that much of America's natural heritage was being damaged by the nation's growth or overuse. He decided to establish a number of conservation programs or acts that would save and preserve nearly 230 million acres of land for all Americans to enjoy. As President he created the U.S. Forest Service in 1905, established 150 National Forests, 51 Federal Bird Reservations, 5 National Parks, and 4 National Game Preserves. His 1906 Antiquities Act also saved 18 National Monuments, such as the Grand Canyon and the Petrified Forest.

On January 11, 1908, Roosevelt declared the Grand Canyon a National Monument.

Family Antics

When the Roosevelt family moved into the White House, all six of the President's children liked to ride bikes, roller skate, and use their stilts throughout the House. The Roosevelt children also had a huge collection of pets, including several dogs; guinea pigs named Admiral Dewey, Dr. Johnson, Bishop Doane, Fighting Bob Evans, and Father O'Grady; a lizard named Bill; Maude the pig; and even a small bear named Jonathan Edwards.

The six Roosevelt children (Ted, Ethel, Alice, Quentin, Kermit, and Archibald) with some of their beloved pets.

Dinner Guest

Roosevelt was the first President to invite an African American man to have dinner at the White House. That man was leader and educator Booker T. Washington. Roosevelt said "...the only wise and honorable and Christian thing to do is to treat each black man and each white man strictly on his merits as a man..."

This picture commemorates Booker T. Washington's White House dinner with the President on October 15, 1901.

EQUALITY

KEY EVENTS

- **September 1901** Roosevelt becomes the 26th President.

- **February 1904** Construction begins on the Panama Canal.

- **February 1905** Roosevelt establishes the National Forest Service.

- **February 1909** The National Association for the Advancement of Colored People is established.

27. WILLIAM HOWARD TAFT

William Taft was a lawyer and judge who became the Secretary of War for Theodore Roosevelt, and then followed him to the presidency. Taft had wanted to continue Roosevelt's improvements, but he liked to think about both sides of an issue, which made him a good judge but an ineffective President. Roosevelt turned against Taft, and even ran against him in the 1912 elections, but they both lost to Woodrow Wilson.

Taft was the first of two Presidents to be buried in Arlington National Cemetery. The other is John F. Kennedy.

The American Game

Taft started the tradition of the presidential "first pitch" of the baseball season on April 4, 1910, at a game between the Washington Senators and the Philadelphia Athletics. Since then, every President except Jimmy Carter has opened at least one baseball season with a "first pitch."

Taft throwing out the first ball, June 9, 1910.

Taft was the first President to have an official White House automobile: a pre-gasoline steam-powered car.

ONE AND ONLY!

Taft is the only man in American history to have held the highest position in both the Executive and Judicial branches of government. He was the President and then the Chief Justice of the Supreme Court.

A Weighty Issue

Weighing more than 300 pounds, Taft was the largest President in American history and was known to get stuck in the White House bathtub. His advisors had to sometimes pull him out. Taft ate a whole steak for breakfast every morning and had a chef at the White House who would make turtle soup for him any time he wanted it. He lost over 75 pounds after he left office.

28. WOODROW WILSON

FAST FACTS

Lived from: 1856–1924
Years in office: 1913–1921
Party: Democratic
VP: Thomas R. Marshall

Considered one of the greatest Presidents of all time, Woodrow Wilson is admired for his vision and accomplishments. During his first term in office, he sought many social improvements, such as regulating the nation's money supply, establishing child labor laws, and enforcing an eight-hour day for railroad workers, all while attempting to keep America out of World War I.

Wilson was given the Nobel Peace Prize for his efforts during World War I.

The Great War in Europe

A global war that lasted from 1914–1918, World War I is know for its devastating loss of life and the huge shifting of empires. Begun when the Archduke Ferdinand of Austria was assassinated, the war pitted the Allied countries of Great Britain, France, and Russia against the Central powers of the Austro-Hungarian Empire, Germany, and the Ottoman Empire. The United States tried to remain neutral (not supporting either side).

The murder of Archduke Ferdinand set off the chain of events that led to World War I.

America and World War I

By Wilson's second term, German submarines attacked American ships and Wilson asked Congress to declare war (1917). The world, he said, must be "made safe for democracy." In January 1919, at the Paris Peace Conference, Wilson, with the help of British, French, and Italian governments, negotiated the Treaty of Versailles to end the war.

The first American troops land on French soil in 1917, ready to fight with the Allies.

Wilson and leaders from 32 nations drafted the Treaty of Versailles in 1919.

THAT'S A FIRST!

Wilson did not learn to read until he was ten, but it seems he did quite a lot of it. Wilson was the first President to have a Ph.D. (a research degree) and to become a professor.

League of Nations

Wilson gave a speech to Congress in 1918 in which he laid out "Fourteen Points" that he believed would prevent future wars. At the end of the "War to End all Wars," as World War I was known, the Treaty of Versailles included many of Wilson's "points," including the idea for a League of Nations. The League was an organization that would settle disputes between countries. In 1920, 42 nations joined the League. Congress refused to ratify the agreement, convinced that they shouldn't get involved in the wars of other countries, so in the end, the United States didn't join.

In 1920, the first session of the League of Nations was held in Geneva, Switzerland.

Women's Suffrage

Suffrage means the right to vote. In 1920, American women gained the right to vote when the Nineteenth Amendment became law. The suffragette movement had been active well before the 1920s, however. Women such as Elizabeth Cady Stanton and Lucretia Mott had been fighting for women's rights for decades. After World War I, the roles that women played in the war were recognized and appreciated, increasing their efforts to gain equality.

VOTES FOR WOMEN

After decades of struggle, American women finally gained the right to vote in 1920.

Wilson's Stroke

Wilson had a stroke while in office in 1919. His wife, Edith, a strong, independent woman who enjoyed driving her own car around Washington, took over much of the behind-the-scenes organization of the presidency while he recuperated. The fact that the President was half-paralyzed was hidden from the nation.

Wilson with his wife, Edith, in 1920, a few months after he had suffered his stroke.

KEY EVENTS

- **March 1913** Wilson becomes the 28th President.

- **June 1914** World War I begins.

- **April 1917** The United States enters World War I.

- **February 1919** Wilson presents his draft of the League of Nations.

- **August 1920** The Nineteenth Amendment gives women the right to vote.

29. WARREN G. HARDING

Warren G. Harding won the first election in which women were allowed to vote. Although considered good-natured, he seemed more interested in being liked than in politics. He filled his cabinet with friends with whom he would play poker, but who also created scandals such as the Teapot Dome incident, that would hurt Harding's reputation. In 1923, Harding suffered a heart attack and died. His Vice President, Calvin Coolidge, was sworn in the next day.

FAST FACTS

Lived from: 1865–1923
Years in office: 1921–1923
Party: Republican
VP: Calvin Coolidge

Harding was a newspaper publisher before becoming President.

THAT'S A FIRST!

Warren Harding was the first President to make a speech over the radio. He was also the first President who knew how to drive.

Mistakes Were Made...

Harding loved to play poker. His advisors were known as the Poker Cabinet and they would play together twice a week. But they also got into trouble. In one such incident, called the Teapot Dome scandal, one of Harding's colleagues illegally gave land to oil companies in exchange for gifts and money. Harding himself was no stranger to mistakes. During one poker match, he bet a set of White House china dating back to Rutherford B. Hayes's administration, and lost it!

This cartoon shows Harding's guilty colleagues trying to outrun the Teapot Dome scandal.

Harding and his wife standing on the back of a train as they leave for their tour of Alaska in 1923.

The Voyage of Understanding

In 1923, while on a tour of the West, Harding became the first American President to visit Alaska, which wouldn't become a state until 1959. (The United States had purchased it from the Russian Empire in 1867.) While on tour, Harding became sick and had to travel back to California.

Harding greets the citizens of Valdez, Alaska, in 1923.

30. CALVIN COOLIDGE

Calvin Coolidge's aim as President was to return the nation to calm, scandal-free times. Nicknamed "Silent Cal" for his quiet nature, Coolidge was a conservative who favored tax cuts, high tariffs on imported goods, and using government funds sparingly. Coolidge's old-fashioned, hands-off presidency was considered comforting during the 1920s, a time of great change.

Coolidge's campaign slogans, such as "keep cool, keep Coolidge," were a sign of the times.

The Roaring Twenties

The 1920s, known as the Roaring Twenties, were a time of enormous lifestyle, technological, and social shifts in America. Jazz music, flappers (dancers), and automobiles all enhanced the mood of the country.

The Charleston became a popular, fashionable dance during the 1920s.

ONE AND ONLY!

Coolidge is the only President to have been born on the 4th of July. Thomas Jefferson (President No. 3), John Adams (President No. 2), and James Monroe (President No. 5) all died on the 4th of July.

Coolidge delivering his first presidential message to Congress in December 1923, following the death of Warren Harding earlier that year.

A Presidential Zoo

Coolidge had the most pets of any President, including two white collies, eight other dogs, canaries, a goose, a mockingbird, cats, two raccoons, a donkey, a bobcat, lion cubs, a bear, a wallaby, and a pygmy hippopotamus. He also had a mechanical horse installed in the White House so he could practice his horseback riding skills!

Coolidge and his wife with two of their dogs in the early 1930s.

31. HERBERT HOOVER

FAST FACTS

Lived from: 1874–1964
Years in office: 1929–1933
Party: Republican
VP: Charles Curtis

When Herbert Hoover became President, he was already well known for organizing aid for Europeans living in poverty after World War I. His focus turned to America, however, after the Stock Market Crash in 1929 set off a period known as the Great Depression. During the next ten years, many Americans lost their jobs and savings and became homeless. But Hoover was unwilling to use government funds to help the poor, believing they should get help from their local communities.

Hoover was nominated five times for the Nobel Peace Prize, in recognition of his humanitarian aid after World War I

THAT'S A FIRST!

Before he became President, Hoover was the first person to appear on television, in an inter-city demonstration of video imagery between Washington, D.C. and New York on April 7, 1927.

The Great Depression

Seven months after Hoover took office, the Stock Market crashed, and people who had put their savings into it lost their money. Businesses failed, leaving people unable to afford their homes. The homeless built shantytowns—known as Hoovervilles— across the country. However, relief wouldn't come until after 1934, when Roosevelt took over the presidency and initiated new reforms.

A Hooverville, or shantytown, built by people who lost their homes in the Depression.

A Presidential Bumble

In 1929, when Hoover was sworn in, he messed up the oath, substituting the word "maintain" for "protect." A 13-year-old from New York wrote to tell him about the error. Since the presidential inauguration was recorded on sound newsreel, the news corporations were able to check that he did, indeed, make a mistake.

Unemployed men line up outside a soup kitchen opened during the Great Depression.

Hoover returning from his inauguration in 1929.

32. FRANKLIN D. ROOSEVELT

FAST FACTS

Lived from: 1882–1945
Years in office: 1933–1945
Party: Democratic
VP: John Nance Garner/
Henry Wallace/
Harry S. Truman

Franklin D. Roosevelt, often known as FDR, is the only President to be elected four times. (After the 22nd Amendment in 1951, the President was limited to two terms.) He took office at a time when, suffering because of the Great Depression, the nation needed consistency, not change. Over the next 12 years, Roosevelt set to work creating ways of solving the nation's troubles. He was also a dominant leader when, from 1939, the world descended into World War II.

Roosevelt entered politics after watching his fifth cousin, Theodore Roosevelt (President No. 26), become President.

Fireside Chats

During the 1930s, no one had a television, but many Americans had radios in their home. Roosevelt wanted to reassure Americans that he was working hard to ease their worries about the Great Depression and World War II. Addressing the people over the radio in his "fireside chats," Roosevelt assured people that they had "nothing to fear but fear itself."

Roosevelt wasn't actually sitting by a fireplace when he gave his "chats."

New Deal

Over his first eight years in office, Roosevelt acted swiftly to try to ease some of the burdens of the Great Depression. He created government programs and projects, known as the New Deal, to get people back to work. His programs funded the building of dams, post offices, bridges, and parks, and gave work to artists and musicians.

The Chickamauga Dam on the Tennessee River was built in the 1930s as part of the New Deal to boost the economy.

FRANKLIN DELANO ROOSEVELT

1882 – 1945

A view of the Franklin D. Roosevelt Monument in the Four Freedoms Park in New York. Roosevelt outlined four freedoms: freedom of speech and worship, and freedom from want or fear.

America and World War II

Two years after the start of World War II, on November 7, 1941, Japanese aircraft dropped bombs on a Hawaiian military base in Pearl Harbor, killing around 2,500 people. The next day, Roosevelt and the U.S. Congress declared that the United States would officially enter the war.

This American battleship was one of many to be destroyed by the Japanese bomb attacks on Pearl Harbor in 1941.

Fourth Term

When Roosevelt was elected to a historic fourth term, the Allies were starting to turn the tide in the war, but Roosevelt's health was failing. He was warned that his heart may not hold out, due to the stresses of running a nation at war, but Roosevelt ran anyway. After only about 100 days in office, he had a stroke and died.

Roosevelt campaigning for his historic fourth term.

KEY EVENTS

- **March 1933** Roosevelt is elected the 33rd President.

- **March 1933** The first "Fireside chat" radio address.

- **September 1939** World War II starts in Europe.

- **December 1941** Japan attacks Pearl Harbor and the United States enters the war.

- **January 1945** Roosevelt begins his fourth term and dies three months later.

Personal Victory

At the age of 39, Roosevelt lost the use of his legs after contracting what the doctors thought was the disease polio (though it's now believed it could have been Guillain–Barré syndrome). Over time, Roosevelt could swim, as well as walk using braces and canes.

Roosevelt spent most of his time using his wheelchair.

First Female Cabinet Member

Roosevelt was the first President to name a woman to his cabinet. Frances Perkins became Secretary of Labor in 1933. She helped to set up the New Deal, and was in charge of changing government laws to reduce accidents in the workplace, ban children from the workforce, and to provide welfare (necessities) for the poor.

Perkins remained in office for Roosevelt's entire presidency.

33. HARRY S. TRUMAN

FAST FACTS

Lived from: 1884–1972
Years in office: 1945–1953
Party: Democratic
VP: Alben Barkley

Following Franklin Roosevelt's death, Vice President Harry S. Truman was sworn in as President. The heavy burden fell on Truman's shoulders to end World War II. The United States had just developed a new weapon—the atomic bomb. Truman made the difficult decision to use the weapon in Japan, to put an end to the war. The bombs were dropped in August 1945 on the towns of Hiroshima and Nagasaki, killing an estimated 200,000 people. Japan surrendered a few days later.

Truman's middle name is just "S." His parents chose "S" in honor of his grandfathers, Solomon Young and Anderson Shipp Truman.

After World War II

Truman signed many bills to help the war-torn European nations rebuild. The Marshall Plan gave money, food, and supplies to Europe. The North Atlantic Treaty Organization (NATO) was a military alliance between 12 countries that promised to protect each other against aggression.

NATO Headquarters in Brussels, Belgium.

The atomic bomb exploding over the Japanese town of Hiroshima in 1945.

Korean War (1950–1953)

In 1950, Communist North Korea invaded South Korea. Truman decided to intervene to help preserve South Korea's independence and stop the spread of Communism. He sent planes, ships, and ground troops to try to halt the North Korean advances. A settlement was reached in 1953 that created a 2-mile-wide no-go zone between the two nations.

U.S. Marines watch artillery fire during the Korean War, 1951

A CLOSE CALL

The 1948 election against Thomas Dewey was so close that many were sure Truman would lose— one newspaper's headline even read "Dewey Defeats Truman."

34. DWIGHT D. EISENHOWER

Eisenhower was a military hero during World War II. He became the commander of President Truman's new NATO force in Europe, and then followed Truman to the presidency. While in office, he increased the **minimum wage** and created the Interstate Highway System, which constructed 41,000 miles of roads across the country.

Dwight "Ike" Eisenhower was the General of the U.S. Army during World War II.

The Cold War

Eisenhower and Soviet Union leader Khrushchev at the White House in 1959.

The Cold War refers to tensions between the Soviet Union (now Russia) and the United States. Although allies during World War II, America distrusted the Communist nation and feared that a build-up of new atomic weapons might lead to war. However, Eisenhower was unable to make a deal with Nikita Khrushchev, the Soviet Premier (leader), to limit weapons testing and continued to expand America's arsenal of weapons.

Brown v. Board of Education decision

In 1954, the Supreme Court decided that public schools should not have "separate but equal" facilities for African American students. This was considered racial **segregation** and unconstitutional. However, one high school in Little Rock, Arkansas, tried to block African American students from enrolling in classes. Eisenhower sent federal troops to escort the students to and from their classes.

African American students attending Little Rock Central High were escorted from class by the U.S. military.

A statue of Eisenhower in Denison, Texas, where he was born in 1890.

ONE AND ONLY!

Dwight D. Eisenhower was the Supreme Commander of the Allied forces during the D-Day invasion of World War II and he is the only President to serve in both World War I and II.

Assassination of the President

On November 22, 1963, Kennedy and the First Lady were in Dallas, Texas, on a campaign trip. They traveled in a motorcade of cars, many of which were convertibles. As their cars drove through Dealey Plaza, three shots were fired; President Kennedy was hit twice. He was rushed to a nearby hospital, where he died soon after.

Kennedy and his wife Jacqueline ride in a motorcade through Dallas in 1963.

Who Did It?

Lee Harvey Oswald, a former Marine who had lived in the Soviet Union, used a rifle to fire on the President from the sixth floor of a school-book warehouse. Two days later, before he could be brought to justice, Oswald was shot and killed by Jack Ruby, a Dallas nightclub owner who supposedly yelled "You killed the President, you rat!"

The shots were supposedly fired from the sixth floor of this building, overlooking the motorcade route.

Other Theories...

Do we know that it was Oswald who shot the President? There have been many other theories, some of which say that there were multiple gunmen, others that it was a government plot, and still others that say evidence had been tampered with. Lyndon B. Johnson, the President after Kennedy, established the Warren Commission to investigate the assassination, but many people believe that we will never truly know what happened.

Lee Harvey Oswald following his arrest for the murder of the President.

KEY EVENTS

- **January 1961** Kennedy becomes the 35th President.

- **April 1961** The Bay of Pigs invasion takes place.

- **October 1962** The Cuban Missile Crisis.

- **August 1963** The March on Washington to support civil rights.

- **November 1963** Kennedy is assassinated in Dallas.

36. LYNDON B. JOHNSON

FAST FACTS

Lived from: 1908–1973
Years in office: 1963–1969
Party: Democratic
VP: Hubert Humphrey

A "larger-than-life" politician, Lyndon Johnson, who was sitting two cars behind Kennedy the day he was shot in Dallas, was sworn in that afternoon. During his terms he signed three civil rights bills, declared a "War on Poverty," and passed a Medicare program (health insurance for people over 65 years old). He wished for the nation to become a "Great Society," one without poverty or injustice.

Lyndon B. Johnson rejected his official portrait painting, saying it was the ugliest thing he ever saw.

LBJ Loved His Initials!

Lyndon Baines Johnson wanted every member of his family to share the same initials (LBJ). His wife's name was Claudia Alta Taylor but she was known as "Lady Bird" Johnson and his two daughters were named Lynda Bird and Luci Baines. Even their dog was named Little Beagle Johnson!

Johnson with his wife, Lady Bird, and daughters Lynda and Luci

Johnson with members of his cabinet at the White House in April 1967.

THAT'S A FIRST!

Johnson was the first President to name an African American to his cabinet. In 1966, he appointed Robert C. Weaver as the head of the Department of Housing and Urban Development, an agency that enforces fair housing laws.

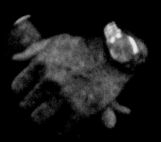

The Vietnam War (1955–1975)

Vietnam was a war of two halves. South Vietnam was ruled by a non-Communist leader. North Vietnam and the Viet Cong (Communist forces) wanted to take over the South and overthrow its leader. Under Johnson, the United States began to operate full-scale missions to help the South Vietnamese.

U.S. soldiers drive into the war zone during the Vietnam War.

37. RICHARD M. NIXON

FAST FACTS

Lived from: 1913–1994
Years in office: 1969–1974
Party: Republican
VP: Spiro Agnew/
Gerald Ford

Richard Nixon spent nearly six years as President before he resigned from (quit) office. During that time he slowly withdrew American troops from Vietnam and reached a peace agreement with North Vietnam. In addition, Nixon signed important new laws about the environment, including ones to reduce car emissions, protect endangered and marine animals, and promote safe drinking water. A massive scandal nicknamed Watergate ended his political career.

Nixon is the only President to have resigned from office.

Nixon enjoying Chinese food with Chinese Premier Zhou Enlai in Beijing in 1972.

Ni hao Nixon, Kak dela?

That means "Hello Nixon" in Chinese and "How are you?" in Russian. Nixon made historic visits to Beijing in China and Moscow in the Soviet Union during his presidency (he was the first President to visit those places). Nixon forged new relationships with the Communist leaders to help reduce tensions and limit the buildup of weapons.

Troops leaving Vietnam to return home to the United States in 1969.

THAT'S A FIRST!

In 1965, Nixon was offered a job with Major League Baseball as a player's representative, but turned it down. "I like the job I have now," he said, "but if I had my life to live over again, I'd like to have ended up a sportswriter."

What's Watergate?

In 1972, people working for Nixon broke into the Watergate Hotel in Washington, D.C., to steal top-secret documents from the Democrats (their opponents). The men were caught, and secret White House conversations that were recorded revealed that Nixon had known about the burglary and tried to cover it up. In August he left the office and Gerald Ford became President.

The Watergate Hotel complex on the Potomac River in Washington, D.C.

38. GERALD FORD

Ford was only President for two and a half years. He gained the office after President Nixon resigned (halfway through his second term), and wasn't reelected in 1976. After the Watergate scandal, Ford needed to convince the American people that politicians and the people who work for the government were hardworking and honest. One of his first acts as President, however, was to pardon (forgive) former President Nixon for any crimes that he may have committed as President.

Ford assumed the presidency under unusual circumstances after Nixon resigned.

Who was Leslie Lynch King Jr.?

That was Gerald Ford's name when he was born. His mother divorced Mr. King when Leslie was a baby. She moved to Michigan and married Gerald R. Ford, who adopted her young son and changed his name. Little "Jerry" grew up to become an all-star football player and was even offered contracts by the Detroit Lions and the Green Bay Packers!

While at the University of Michigan, Ford played center for the Wolverines football team.

THAT'S A FIRST!

Ford was the first to be both Vice President and President without being elected. Spiro Agnew, the Vice President under Nixon, resigned, so Ford was appointed Vice President. He then rose to President when Nixon left office.

The U.S. and the U.S.S.R. in Space

Relations on Earth between America and the Soviet Union were shaky during Ford's presidency, but not in space! In 1975, a U.S. Apollo spacecraft carrying three astronauts docked with a Soviet spacecraft. Known as the Apollo-Soyuz Test Project, it was the first international partnership in space.

The American crew of the Apollo-Soyuz Test Project lift off from Kennedy Space Center in 1975, to join the Russians in space.

39. JIMMY CARTER

FAST FACTS

Lived from: 1924–
Years in office: 1977–1981
Party: Democratic
VP: Walter Mondale

Jimmy Carter was born and raised on a peanut farm in Georgia. He was respected for being honest, hardworking, and a "man of the people." While in the White House, he helped negotiate a peace agreement, known as the Camp David Accords, between the warring countries of Israel and Egypt. He also tried to free 66 U.S. hostages held in Iran for 444 days. (They were released the day he left office.)

Carter was the first President to be born in a hospital rather than at home.

Energy Crisis

In the 1970s, Americans used a lot of oil, especially gasoline. When the Middle Eastern countries that supplied the oil decided to stop importing it to the United States, the price of fuel skyrocketed. Americans couldn't afford to fill their gas tanks. Carter encouraged the establishment of other forms of energy, like solar, wind, or nuclear power.

In 1979, people would wait hours to fill up their tanks.

Carter encouraged peace between Egyptian President Anwar Sadat (left) and Israeli Prime Minister Menachem Begin (right).

Post-Presidency

Carter has done some extraordinary things since he left the presidency: he works for Habitat for Humanity, an organization that builds houses for underprivileged people; he's written 28 books; he founded a nonprofit center to encourage democracy and human rights around the world; and he continues to help negotiate peace between nations at war. In 2002, he was awarded the Nobel Peace Prize for his accomplishments.

Carter spends one week every year at a construction site to build affordable houses.

40. RONALD REAGAN

FAST FACTS

Lived from: 1911–2004
Years in office: 1981–1989
Party: Republican
VP: George H.W. Bush

Ronald Reagan was known as the "Great Communicator" for his skillful ability to talk about issues. He was an actor who starred in 53 Hollywood films before changing careers to become governor and then President. Reagan felt that if Americans had more money in their pockets they would spend more money, which would increase the wealth and well-being of the country. He was also known for wanting to put weapons in space to protect Americans from attacks from the Soviet Union.

Reagan was twice named *Time* magazine's "Man of the Year," in 1980 and 1984.

Superpowers

America and the Soviet Union were known as two "superpowers" during the Cold War. This means that both countries had atomic weapons and greater influence in the world than most other nations. Reagan met with Mikhail Gorbachev, the leader of the Soviet Union, to try to end the Cold War peacefully.

Reagan and Gorbachev worked tirelessly to eliminate nuclear weapons, rather than just limit them.

ONE AND ONLY!

Reagan was 69 when he was elected President, which makes him the oldest person ever elected. He was also the first President to appoint a woman (Sandra Day O'Connor) to the U.S. Supreme Court.

The Berlin Wall

In the 1960s, a huge wall was built in the German city of Berlin to keep people from leaving the Communist East to join the Democratic West. In 1987, Reagan gave a speech to "Tear down this wall!" Two years later, on November 9, 1989, protesters in Germany chiseled away at the wall and were finally free to cross the border. Reagan even took some swings of the hammer!

East Germans listening to a speech given by Reagan at the Brandenburg Gate near the Berlin Wall on June 12, 1987.

Berlins
Reagan
me
esident!

41. GEORGE H.W. BUSH

FAST FACTS

Lived from: 1924–
Years in office: 1989–1993
Party: Republican
VP: Dan Quayle

The world was rapidly changing when George H.W. Bush was President—the Cold War ended, the Berlin Wall fell, and the Communist Soviet Union broke apart. However, it would be another war—the Persian Gulf War—that would take up much of Bush's focus. He was also known for signing two important bills: the Americans with Disabilities Act, making it illegal to treat people with disabilities unfairly; and the Clean Air Act, to reduce the amount of pollution in the air.

George Herbert Walker Bush is the only President with four names.

First Gulf War

When the country of Iraq, led by Saddam Hussein, invaded the neighboring country of Kuwait, President Bush joined with the leaders of the United Kingdom and the Soviet Union to help Kuwait. The war, known in the United States as Operation Desert Storm, began in January 1991 and lasted for two months before Kuwait was freed.

Saddam Hussein, President of Iraq, invaded Kuwait in August 1990.

No Broccoli!

Bush banned broccoli aboard the presidential airplane Air Force One. He is reported to have said: "I haven't liked it since I was a little kid and my mother made me eat it. And I'm President of the United States, and I'm not going to eat any more broccoli!"

Bush and his wife visiting U.S. troops in Saudi Arabia in 1990.

Bush developed a lifelong dislike of broccoli.

THAT'S A FIRST!

Bush celebrated his 75th birthday by jumping out of a plane—he was skydiving, of course. Then he did it again on his 80th, 85th, and even his 90th birthdays!

THE 2000S

In the 21st century, technology and the rise of social media have changed the way humans interact.

2002 Bluetooth technology is introduced as the first peer-to-peer wireless technology.

2004 Facebook is launched, and social networking becomes a global phenomenon.

2000 — **2002** — **2004** — **2006**

2001 On September 11, four hijacked airplanes crash, killing over 3,000 people.

2003 The human genome project is completed, helping scientists understand the structure of human DNA.

2006 Former Vice President Al Gore's filmed lecture "An Inconvenient Truth" about global warming opens in the United States and goes on to win two Oscars.

2000 The segway, a two-wheeled electronic scooter, is produced.

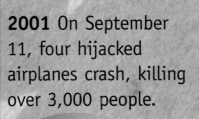

2001 The first robotic artificial heart is made. (It worked on a battery pack strapped to the user's waist, and lasted five months, much longer than expected.)

2001 The iPod, Apple's version of the MP3 player, is born.

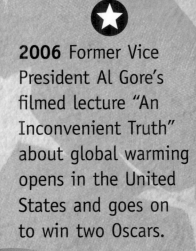

2003 Two rovers, named Spirit and Opportunity, begin their exploration of the planet Mars.

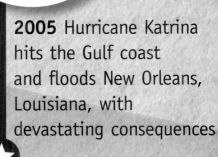

2005 Hurricane Katrina hits the Gulf coast and floods New Orleans, Louisiana, with devastating consequences.

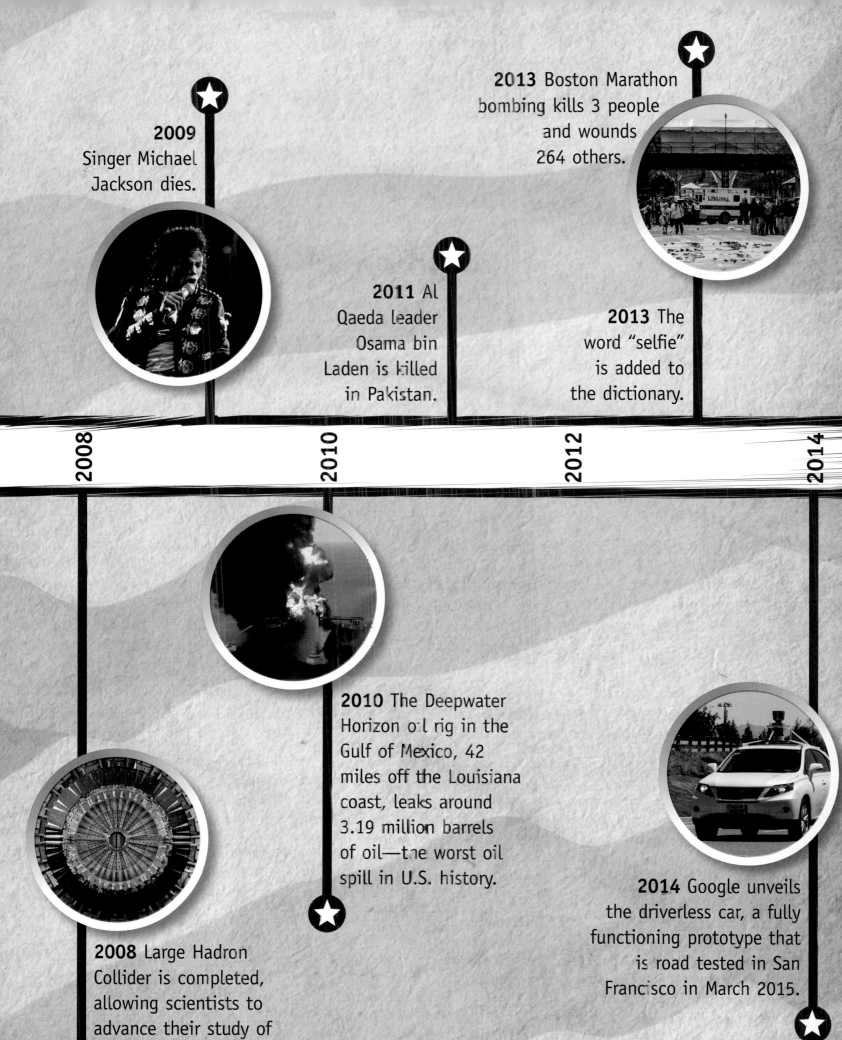

2009 Singer Michael Jackson dies.

2013 Boston Marathon bombing kills 3 people and wounds 264 others.

2011 Al Qaeda leader Osama bin Laden is killed in Pakistan.

2013 The word "selfie" is added to the dictionary.

2008

2010

2012

2014

2010 The Deepwater Horizon oil rig in the Gulf of Mexico, 42 miles off the Louisiana coast, leaks around 3.19 million barrels of oil—the worst oil spill in U.S. history.

2008 Large Hadron Collider is completed, allowing scientists to advance their study of particle physics.

2014 Google unveils the driverless car, a fully functioning prototype that is road tested in San Francisco in March 2015.

44. BARACK OBAMA

Barack Obama is the first African American President of the United States. He became President after spending eight years in the Illinois state government and three years as a U.S. senator. Since being President, Obama has pushed for higher taxes, passed a new healthcare act, and has withdrawn U.S. troops from Iraq.

FAST FACTS

Lived from: 1961–
Years in office: 2009–2017
Party: Democratic
VP: Joe Biden

Obama, President No. 44, won a second term in office in 2012.

Affordable Care Act

One of the biggest pieces of legislation that Obama introduced was the Affordable Care Act, a healthcare policy intended to help poor people afford health insurance. This means that people who couldn't afford to go to doctors or pay for medical treatments could receive care. Since 2010, more than 16 million Americans have received health coverage under the new act.

Supporters at a 2012 rally for healthcare.

On January 20, 2009, an estimated two million people stood outside the Capitol Building in Washington, D.C., to hear Obama's inaugural speech.

Obama with his mother and half sister in Indonesia, where he spent his childhood.

Family Life

Obama was born in Hawaii to an American mother and a Kenyan father. His parents divorced and he moved to Indonesia with his mother. When he was ten he returned to Hawaii to live with his grandparents. Obama enjoyed being raised as a child of numerous cultures. "I was raised as an Indonesian child, and a Hawaiian child, and as a black child, and as a white child." he said.

Financial Woes

Obama's presidential career began, like Roosevelt's and Reagan's, during a time of financial conflict. The economy wasn't growing and the nation's banks and car companies were in danger of collapsing. Many people were out of work and couldn't afford their houses. Obama lent government money to the failing companies and saved them. In 2009, he signed the American Recovery and Reinvestment Act, which gave money to the states to provide jobs and cut taxes.

Obama, with Vice President Joe Biden, signing the American Recovery and Reinvestment Act in 2009.

Award Season

Obama has won both a Grammy—for the audio version of his book *The Audacity of Hope*—and a Nobel Peace Prize (2009)— for his "vision of and work for a world without nuclear weapons." Two other Presidents have won Grammy Awards: Bill Clinton and Jimmy Carter.

Obama is the fourth U.S. President (after Theodore Roosevelt, Woodrow Wilson, and Jimmy Carter) to win the Nobel Peace Prize.

A New Policy in Cuba

Events known as the Bay of Pigs and the Cuban Missile Crisis of the 1960s (see page 103) had soured the relationship between the United States and the island of Cuba. For the past 50 years, Americans were restricted from visiting Cuba or trading with the island. Obama and Raul Castro, Cuba's President, have reestablished a relationship between the two countries, which will hopefully be beneficial to both nations.

Obama and Raul Castro at a meeting in April 2015.

KEY EVENTS

- **January 2009** Obama becomes the 44th President.

- **March 2010** Obama signs the Affordable Care Act into law.

- **May 2011** Bin Laden is killed.

- **November 2012** Obama wins his second term in office.

- **January 2015** The Republicans control both houses of Congress.

VOTING

Every four years, Americans choose who will be the next President by participating in an election. There are two steps to the election process: a primary election and a general election. In the primary, candidates compete to be the leader of a party, such as the Democratic Party. In the general, the party leaders' names are placed on a **ballot** so that Americans can vote for the one they think will be the best person to run the country.

A ballot from the 2012 presidential election.

PRESIDENT AND VICE-
OF THE UNITED STATES
e for not more than 1

Mitt Romney
Paul Ryan
Republican

Barack Obama
Joe Biden
Democratic

POLLING

PLACE

Citizens line up to vote at their local polling station.

The General Election

In a general election, each state counts the votes in its state and declares a state winner, who is then given a number of electoral votes—the number depends on how many members of Congress come from that state. There are 538 total electoral votes across the 50 states and Washington, D.C. The candidate who wins at least 270 of them becomes President of the United States.

Barack Obama at his election victory in 2008.

Winning the Election but NOT Becoming President

In the United States it is possible to win the most total votes but not become President. In 2000, more people voted for Democratic Leader Al Gore than for Republican George W. Bush. However, Bush became President because he won in more states and had more electoral votes (271) than Gore (266). Three other Presidents have won this way: John Quincy Adams, Rutherford B. Hayes, and Benjamin Harrison.

This map shows the states that voted for Bush in red, and the states that voted for Gore in blue during the 2000 presidential election.

Will the next President be YOU?

Don't forget that you have to be 35 or older to become President. But there are no restrictions on what race, color, sex, or religion you have to be. Will the next President be a woman? There have been female leaders in many countries across the world—for instance Germany, the United Kingdom, and Australia. Perhaps the next U.S. President will be one, too.

Former First Lady Hillary Clinton is running in the 2016 presidential race.

Voting is a right and an opportunity to participate in a democracy.

John F. Kennedy and Richard Nixon running for President in 1960.

Winners and Losers

Only one person can be President at a time, but losing an election doesn't mean the candidate can't run again in four years' time. A quarter of the Presidents have lost an election and gone on to win it later on. For example, Richard Nixon lost to John F. Kennedy in the 1960 election, but won the presidency eight years later.

How to Vote

Every American citizen over the age of 18 is eligible to vote. First you will need to register (sign up) in the state in which you live. Every state has different laws about how to do this. Each state sets up polling stations—places people can go on Election Day to "cast a ballot," or choose whom they would like for President. Or you can mail in your vote!

A voter casts his ballot at a polling station.

Why Voting Matters

The United States is a democracy, meaning it has a system of government in which each person has a say in how the country should be run. But we can't all live at the White House, so we vote in order to elect people to represent each one of us and our beliefs. Voting matters because the people we vote for are the ones who will be creating laws and making important decisions that affect our lives—decisions about things like the environment, schools, and our safety.

Rock the Vote, founded in 1990, is an organization that encourages young Americans to vote.

FIRST LADIES

Martha Washington

1 Martha was the first historical woman to appear on banknotes.

Abigail Adams

2 Abigail was the first First Lady to live in the White House.

Martha Jefferson

3 Martha died before Jefferson became President in 1801.

Dolley Madison

4 Dolley often wore her parrot on her shoulder to wow her guests.

Elizabeth Monroe

5 With her family, Elizabeth spoke only in French.

Louisa Adams

6 Louisa was born outside of the United States, in England.

Rachel Jackson

7 Rachel married Andrew before she was divorced from her first husband.

Hannah Van Buren

8 Hannah died before Martin Van Buren became President.

Anna Harrison

9 Anna married William Henry in secret, against her father's wishes.

Letitia Tyler

(10) Letitia was the first First Lady to die in the White House.

Julia Tyler

(10) Two years after Letitia's death, President Tyler married Julia.

Sarah Polk

(11) Sarah Polk refused to allow dancing at the White House.

Margaret "Peggy" Taylor

(12) Peggy learned to shoot when she lived on the Western frontier.

Abigail Fillmore

(13) Abigail began the first official library in the Executive Mansion.

Jane Pierce

(14) Mourning the death of her young son, Jane only wore black.

None*

(15) Harriet Lane, Buchanan's niece, assumed First Lady duties.

Mary Lincoln

(16) Mary held seances (ceremonies) to contact dead loved ones.

Eliza Johnson

(17) Eliza taught Andrew Johnson arithmetic and spelling.

Julia Grant

(18) Julia owned slaves while Ulysses served in the Union Army.

Lucy Hayes

(19) Lucy was the first First Lady to earn a college degree.

Lucretia Garfield

(20) Lucretia, a teacher, married one of her students, James Garfield.

*James Buchanan never married.

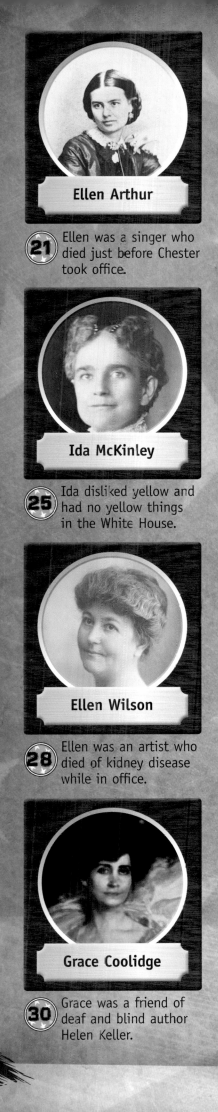

Ellen Arthur

21 Ellen was a singer who died just before Chester took office.

Frances Cleveland

22 & 24 Frances was First Lady twice. Grover won two terms in 1885 and 1893.

Caroline Harrison

23 Caroline was the first to have a Christmas tree in the White House.

Ida McKinley

25 Ida disliked yellow and had no yellow things in the White House.

Edith Roosevelt

26 Edith raised six children and several pets at the White House.

Helen "Nellie" Taft

27 Nellie was the first First Lady to own and drive a car.

Ellen Wilson

28 Ellen was an artist who died of kidney disease while in office.

Edith Wilson

28 Edith was a direct descendant of Pocahontas.

Florence Harding

29 Florence invited scientist Marie Curie to the White House.

Grace Coolidge

30 Grace was a friend of deaf and blind author Helen Keller.

Lou Hoover

31 Lou spoke Chinese, having once lived in China with her husband.

Eleanor Roosevelt

32 Eleanor once flew in a plane with aviator Amelia Earhart.

Bess Truman

33 Bess Truman never gave an interview as First Lady.

Mamie Eisenhower

34 Mamie was outgoing and loved feminine clothes and jewelry.

Jacqueline Kennedy

35 Jacqueline interviewed Kennedy in 1951, and married him in 1953!

Claudia Johnson

36 "Lady Bird" founded the Lady Bird Johnson Wildflower Center.

Pat Nixon

37 Pat was the first First Lady to earn a graduate degree.

Betty Ford

38 Betty worked as a dancer with the Martha Graham Company.

Rosalynn Carter

39 Rosalynn was described as a "steel magnolia": sweet but strong.

Nancy Reagan

40 The Secret Service gave Nancy the code name "Rainbow."

Barbara Bush

41 Barbara wrote *C. Fred's Story* and *Millie's Book* about her dogs.

Hillary Clinton

42 Hillary is the only First Lady to run for President herself.

Laura Bush

43 Laura gave a weekly presidential radio address while in office.

Michelle Obama

44 Michelle, a lawyer, launched the program Let's Move! to address childhood obesity.

HALLMARKS OF A NATION

Liberty Bell, 1753

The Pennsylvania State House, now known as Independence Hall, wanted to install a bell. One was made in 1752 in London, England, but it cracked. In 1753, a new bell was cast from the metal of the old bell and hung in the tower of Independence Hall. The Liberty Bell is inscribed with the words "Proclaim Liberty Throughout All the Land Unto All the Inhabitants thereof."

The bell is a mix of copper, tin, zinc, lead, arsenic, silver, and gold. It weighs about 2,000 pounds (1 ton).

U.S. and Presidential Seals, 1782

A seal is a symbol of our nation that appears on official documents. The design has gone through many changes but it now has an eagle carrying 13 arrows in one talon and an olive branch in the other. In its beak is a scroll with the Latin words *E Pluribus Unum*, which means "Out of Many, One." (Meaning out of many colonies, one nation emerged.)

The first President who used a presidential seal (based on the national seal) was Rutherford B. Hayes in 1880.

The Bald Eagle, 1782

When the Founding Fathers discussed what should be the national symbol, some chose the golden eagle, and others, such as Benjamin Franklin, wanted the wild turkey. But in the end, the American Bald Eagle was selected. The bald eagle can be seen on the Seals of the United States, on coins and paper money, and on postage stamps. The bald eagle was included on the endangered species list in 1967 but was removed in 2007.

The national bird is the only eagle unique to North America.

Uncle Sam, 1813

Samuel Wilson was a meatpacker who sent barrels of beef to the army during the War of 1812. When asked why the barrels had the letters "U.S." on them, one man supposedly joked that it stood for "Uncle Sam" Wilson. Over time, Uncle Sam came to be thought of as the U.S. government.

This 1917 army poster made the image of Uncle Sam famous.

The national anthem is sung at major sporting events.

Star-Spangled Banner, 1814

The "Star-Spangled Banner" is the national anthem, or national song, of the United States. Francis Scott Key, an American lawyer, wrote the words in 1814 after watching a battle between Great Britain and America at Fort McHenry, in Baltimore, Maryland.

GLOSSARY

Abolitionist A person who wants to abolish, or end, slavery.

Amendments Changes or additions made to the Constitution.

American Revolution From 1775 to 1783, American colonists fought against, and overthrew, the British who were ruling them, and founded the United States of America.

Annexation Addition of an area or region to a country.

Assassinated Deliberately killed for political or monetary reasons.

Ballot A system of voting using a paper card or an electronic ticket to choose a winner.

Bill of Rights The first ten additions to the Constitution, giving individuals certain rights under the law.

Bills Laws that haven't been agreed on or passed yet.

Cabinet A group of advisers to the President.

Candidates People nominated to run in an election.

Checks and balances A system created to divide power between different branches of government, so that none is more powerful than the others.

Citizens Members of a certain country.

Colonies New territories that are ruled by another country.

Communist A person or group that follows a system in which the government owns and produces things and wealth is divided equally among all people.

Confederacy A group of 11 states that seceded, or left, the Union during the American Civil War. Also known as the South. See **Union**.

Congress A group of men and women who are elected to the Senate and the House of Representatives, and make up the Legislative Branch of the government.

Conservative Valuing traditional practices rather than change. See **Liberal**.

Constitution A document containing the beliefs and laws of a country.

Continental Divide A chain of mountains that runs north to south through all of North America.

Declaration of Independence A document that announced that the 13 American colonies would become an independent nation and would no longer be part of the British Empire.

Democracy A system whereby the government is run by the people, or by representatives elected by the people.

Depression A long or severe dip or downturn in a nation's economy, resulting in unemployment and the loss of businesses; in 1929 it was known as the Great Depression.

Desegregation See **Segregation**

Economic Relating to a financial (monetary) system in which products are bought and sold.

Elect To choose a person or group by voting.

Federal The central, national government (as opposed to the government run by each state).

Founding Fathers of America A group of men from the colonies in America who revolted against the authority of the British crown and founded, or started, a new nation.

Government The system of rules for a country, and the people who make them.

Great Depression See **Depression**

House of Representatives A group of elected officials that, along with the Senate, makes up the Congress.

Impeached Charged an official, such as the President, with a crime.

Inauguration The formal ceremony that introduces a person to his or her new job.

Liberal Not sticking with the traditional ways of doing things; and believing that government should be active in supporting social change.

Minimum wage The lowest hourly or daily fee that employees can pay to workers.

Monarchy A form of government in which there is one ruler who rules until death.

Nationalist A person who supports political independence for their country.

Policy Plan of action proposed by the government.

Ratify To sign or agree to a document, making it official or valid.

Reconstruction Putting the country back together after a war.

Secede To separate from a nation and become independent.

Segregation The practice of keeping people of different races separate from each other.

Sue To take someone to court or take legal action against someone.

Tariffs Charging money for things going into or out of a country.

Tax A fee charged by the government on its citizens.

Terms Limited time in which a government official may serve in office.

Terrorists A group of people who use violence to frighten others, usually as a way of achieving a goal.

Underground Railroad A network of secret hiding places created by people who helped fugitive slaves escape to the North.

Unemployed A person who does not have a job.

Union, The During the Civil War, the Union was made up of the national government and the states that supported it. Also known as the North. See **Confederacy**.

Veto The power to reject or say no to a bill.

INDEX

Picture Credits

Key: t = top, b = bottom, c = center, l = left, r = right

Alamy: 3 World History Archive, 9br North Wind Picture Archives, 10br PAINTING, 11bl Everett Collection Historical, 11br dbimages, 13br Ron Buskirk, 14(3) GL Archive, 14(8) North Wind Picture Archives, 15(10) Niday Picture Library, 15(11) GL Archive, 15(13) Niday Picture Library, 15(14) GL Archive, 15(15) dbimages, 15(17) dbimages, 15(18) North Wind Picture Archives, 15(20) PAINTING, 15(21) Niday Picture Library, 16(23) Niday Picture Library, 16(27) North Wind Picture Archives, 16(28) World History Archive, 16(30) Heritage Image Partnership Ltd, 16(31) Glasshouse Images, 17(34) Heritage Image Partnership Ltd, 17(37) World History Archive, 17(38) GL Archive, 17(39) Glasshouse Images, 17(40) GL Archive, 17(41) Ian Shaw, 18cl North Wind Picture Archives, 19tcr Old Paper Studios, 19tcl Pictorial Press Ltd, 19tl Lebrecht Music and Arts Photo Library, 22br North Wind Picture Archives, 24–25 ClassicStock, 25tr World History Archive, 26cr North Wind Picture Archives, 27tr The Protected Art Archive, 27tl The Protected Art Archive, 27cl Everett Historica. Collection, 28cl GL Archive, 28–29 GL Archive, 31br North Wind Picture Archives, 33cr PAINTING, 36–37 North Wind Picture Archives, 38cr North Wind Picture Archives, 40br Susan Pease, 40–41 North Wind Picture Archives, 42bl North Wind Picture Archives, 42–43 Bygone Collection, 44tl Niday Picture Library, 44–45 PRISMA ARCHIVO, 45tr Niday Picture Library, 46cl GL Archive, 46–47 Chronicle, 47cr North Wind Picture Archives, 48bl North Wind Picture Archives, 48–49 Classic Image, 49br Bygone Collection, 50bl PAINTING, 50–51 Niday Picture Library, 51bl North Wind Picture Archives, 52br Pictorial Press Ltd, 52cl GL Archive, 54bl dbimages, 54–55 Universal Images Group Limited, 55tl Everett Collection Historical, 58bl North Wind Picture Archives, 60cl dbimages, 61br North Wind Picture Archives, 62cl North Wind Picture Archives, 63cr North Wind Picture Archives, 66cl PAINTING, 68tl Historical image collection by Bildagentur-online, 68–69 Niday Picture Library, 70–71 North Wind Picture Archives, 71br North Wind Picture Archives, 72–73 Niday Picture Library, 74cl Everett Collection Historical, 74br North Wind Picture Archives, 74–75 North Wind Picture Archives, 76cr The Art Archive, 76–77 Nicay Picture Library, 79bc Pictorial Press Ltd, 79bl ZUMA Press, Inc., 79tcl White House Photo, 80–81 GL Archive, 81cl Robert Harding Picture Library Ltd, 82br North Wind Picture Archives, 83tr Pictorial Press Ltd, 84cl North Wind Picture Archives, 86br akg-images, 36cl World History Archive, 87cr Trinity Mirror/Mirrorpix, 92–93 Everett Collection Historical, 93bl Heritage Image Partnership Ltd, 94bl Glasshouse Images, 95tl The Art Archive, 96br Everett Collection Historical, 96–97 Richard Green, 98bl Everett Collection Historical, 98–99 Nicay Picture Library, 99tl Everett Collection Historical, 100bl Agencja Fotograficzna Caro, 100–101 World History Archive, 102cl Heritage Image Partnership Ltd, 102br Everett Collection Historical, 105cr History Archives, 106–107 RGB Ventures/Superstock, 107tl Mug Shot, 110cl World History Archive, 112tl GL Archive, 113br RGB Ventures/SuperStock, 114tl Glasshouse Images, 116br World History Archive, 116cl GL Archive, 116–117 Sueddeutsche Zeitung Photo, 117cr imageBROKER, 113bl peter jordan, 118cr Ian Shaw, 120–121 History Archives, 121br Historic Florida, 123bl VIEW Pictures Ltd, 123br SiliconValleyStock, 124–125 Trinity Mirror/Mirrorpix, 125br The Protected Art Archive, 127tr ZUMA Press Inc., 129cr Xinhua, 130–131 Rob Crandall, 131br Elvele Images Ltd, 133br Richard Levine 7, 134(3) ClassicStock, 134(4) Everett Collection Historical, 134(5) Everett Collection Historical, 134(6) North Wind Picture Archives, 134(7) Everett Collection Historical, 135(10tl) Everett Collection Historical, 135(10tc) Universal Images Group Limited, 135(11) Everett Collection Historical, 135(13) Everett Collection Historical, 135(14) Niday Picture Library, 135(17) North Wind Picture Archives, 136(22&24) Everett Collection Historical, 136(23) Classic Image, 136(26) Everett Collection Historical, 136(27) Everett Collection Historical, 136(30) Glasshouse Images, 137(33) Everett Collection Historical, 137(35) Pictorial Press Ltd, 137(36) Everett Collection Historical, 137(39) Everett Collection Historical, 137(44) White House Photo, 139cl Warships.

Bridgeman Images: 19tr American Antiquarian Society, Worcester, Massachusetts, USA.

Corbis: 7tl, 12tr KEVIN LAMARQUE/Reuters, 14(4), 15(19), 16(25), 16(26), 16(32) Oscar White, 16(33) GraphicaArtis, 17(35), 17(36) Bettmann, 19br, 21tr Glen Stubbe/ZUMA Press, 22–23, 31tr Hal Horwitz, 32cl, 34–35, 37cr, 38bl National Geographic Creative, 45br Dave G. Houser. 46br Bettmann, 60–61, 64cl, 64br, 65br Chris Hellier, 66br, 66–67, 67br Lebrecht Authors/Lebrecht Music & Arts/Lebrecht Music & Arts/Corbis, 70br Leonard de Selva, 76bl, 77cr, 79tcr Bettmann, 80cl, 84–85, 88–89 Hulton-Deutsch Collection, 90–91, 91br, 92cl Bettmann, 96tl Oscar White, 99br, 100tc GraphicaArtis, 103cr Bettmann, 104br Bettmann 104–105 Bettmann, 108br Bettmann, 108cl, 108–109 Bettmann, 110bl Bettmann, 110–111 Bettmann, 112br Bettmann, 114–115 Historical, 115bl Mark Peterson, 118–119 Wally McNamee, 128–129 LARRY DOWNING/Reuters, 132bl Bettmann, 132tr Reuters, 135(12) Bettmann, 135(16), 136(31), 137(34) Bettmann, 137(38) Douglas Kirkland, 137(40) Douglas Kirkland, 137(42) Jeffrey Markowitz/Sygma, 137(43) Martin H. Simon.

David Rumsey Map Collection: 23tr.

Getty Images: 8bl National Archives/The LIFE Picture Collection, 12bl DeAgostini, 14(2) DeAgostini, 14(5) DeAgostini, 14(6) DeAgostini, 17(42) PAUL J. RICHARDS/AFP, 18bc Buyenlarge, 19bc MPI, 24c DeAgostini, 28bl MPI, 34tl DeAgostini, 36tl, DeAgostini, 78c Apic, 79cl SSPL, 79cr FABRICE COFFRINI/AFP, 79tl Patrick Christian, 81cr Farrell Grehan/National Geographic, 84br Transcendental Graphics, 89tr Underwood Archives, 97cr Panoramic Images, 101br MPI/Hulton Archive, 109cr Co Rentmeester/The LIFE Picture Collection, 114bl Warren Leffler/Underwood Archives, 120tl PAUL J. RICHARDS/AFP, 120br Arnold Sachs, 122cl Segway, 123tl Kevin Mazur/WireImage, 123tr Photo by Aram Boghosian for The Boston Globe via Getty Images, 128br JEWEL SAMAD/AFP, 130bl Andy Sacks, 135(15) Hulton Archive, 137(37) Bachrach.

iStockphoto: 132–133 maley099.

Library of Congress: 6bl, 6–7, 11tl, 15(12), 16(29), 17(43), 17(44), 18cr, 24bl, 26bl, 32br, 32–33, 35tr, 41br, 48cl, 62–63, 68br, 73cr, 78bl, 88br, 90bl, 95br, 102–103, 112–113, 124bl, 126bl, 134(9), 135(20), 136(21), 136(25), 136(28r), 136(29), 136(32), 137(41) Cynthia Johnson/The LIFE Images Collection.

NASA: 122bcr.

Rex Features: 86–87, 92br, 127cl Barney Henderson.

Shutterstock: fc, 4bl Richard Laschon, 5tr Everett Historical, 5bl Marquestra, 8tl dibrova, 9tl Everett Historical, 9tc Everett Historical, 9tr alphaspirit, 9cr HitToon.com, 10cl Everett Historical, 11tr Drop of Light, 13bl annt, 13cl AridOcean, 13cr Mark Van Scyoc, 13c Everett Historical, 14(1) CrackerClips Stock Media, 14(7) Everett Historical, 14(9) Everett Historical, 15(16) Everett Historical, 16(22) Everett Historical, 16(24) Everett Historical, 19bl Everett Historical, 20br Vladimir Wrangel, 20cl Everett Historical, 20–21 CrackerClips Stock Media, 27cr Don Mammoser, 27br Norgal, 27tc Everett Historical, 29cr Everett Historical, 30br Joseph Sohm, 30–31 Daniel M. Silva, 36br Jon Bilous, 38–39 Everett Historical, 39cr Everett Historical, 42c Everett Historical, 43br Everett Historical, 53cr Everett Historical, 55br Everett Historical, 56cl Everett Historical, 56br Everett Historical, 56–57 Brandon Bourdages, 57cr Everett Historical, 58–59 Everett Historical, 59tr Everett Historical, 62br Everett Historical, 70cl Everett Historical, 72cl Linda Armstrong, 73bl Terence Mendoza, 75cr Hein Nouwens, 78bcl Keith Tarrier, 78bcr Everett Historical, 78cr Everett Historical, 82–83 sumikophoto, 94–95 Everett Historical, 106br Joseph Sohm, 111br Frontpage, 119cr makeitdouble, 122tr tulpahn, 122br imagist, 122bcl Anthony Correia, 126–127 Paul Hakimata Photography, 131tr Everett Collection, 133tr Joseph Sohm, 134(1) Everett Historical, 134(2) Everett Historical, 134(8) Everett Historical, 135(18) Everett Historical, 135(19) Everett Historical, 136(28l) Everett Historical, 138bl Richard Laschon, 138tc Songquan Deng, 139tr Marquestra, 139br Everett Historical.

Topfoto: 34bl The Granger Collection, 40cl The Granger Collection, 52–53 The Granger Collection, 64–65 The Granger Collection, 69cr The Granger Collection, 91tr The Granger Collection.

US Coastguard: 123cl.

Author Acknowledgements: A huge thank you to everyone at Calcium Creative, including Amanda Learmonth, Sarah Eason, and Paul Myerscough for their dedication and hard work. And another massive thanks to the whole team at QED, especially Vicky Garrard for asking me to write this book and Sophie Hallam for all her editorial skills. This book is for my PAJAMA family and TEZSHN (all our new recruits!)